TARA: CHILD OF HOPES & DREAMS

TARA: CHILD OF HOPES & DREAMS

by Donna Nason

TYNDALE HOUSE
PUBLISHERS, INC.
WHEATON, ILLINOIS

*Library of Congress
Catalog Card Number
78-54087
ISBN 0-8423-6920-1, paper*

*First printing,
July 1978.
Printed in the
United States of America.*

Dedicated to the glory of God
and to my husband

M I C H A E L

without whose encouragement
this book would never have
been written.

CONTENTS

ACKNOWLEDGMENTS

I wish to express my sincere gratitude for the support several people have given me during the writing of this book. A special thank-you goes to my mother Claire Henson and to Marge Kurz for their unselfish giving of countless hours to type the manuscript; and to Terry Patané, who upheld this project in prayer.

I am also indebted to Patricia Moriarity, who cared for the children while I wrote; and to Tara's daily team captains: Iris Bjorklund, Shirley Garcia, Esther Gash, Sonia Scott, and Kathleen Witt, who lovingly continued her program while I was away.

A note of thanks also goes to Tony Palladino, who generously donated his time to build Tara's Spring Turtle.

CHAPTER ONE
Baby, Baby

Shafts of sunlight streamed through the open windows of our second-floor bedroom. Outside the birds were singing their late summer songs. Mike lay next to me in bed, curled up, still sound asleep. The rhythmic sound of his breathing was peaceful, lulling me.

From downstairs I could hear our ten-year-old son Mark beginning to stir, rolling quickly from side to side in his bed and singing. High-pitched peals of little-girl laughter drifted in from the next room. "Uh-oh," I whispered sleepily to myself. "Christa's climbed out of her crib again and has wakened Tara. We won't be able to stay in bed much longer now."

As if in answer to my thoughts, a pair of enormous, bright blue eyes peeked into the room. Then a rush of tiny feet and short, stubby legs came toddling over to the bed. I pretended to be asleep, sneaking a look between partially closed lashes. Christa bent over and brushed her blonde curls against Mike's cheek. "Daddy," she began in her husky little voice, all the while poking at him through the blankets for emphasis, "Tara go potty."

Drowsily, Mike opened first one eye and then the other. "OK, OK," he mumbled. "Tell her I'll be there in a minute." He reached sleepily for his blue terry cloth robe and shuffled into Tara's bedroom. I could hear him strain as he lifted seven-year-old Tara onto his shoulders and carried her into the bathroom.

"I only woke you up once last night, Daddy," she bubbled with characteristic enthusiasm.

"Twice," Mike corrected, "once to go potty and once to adjust your leg."

"Oh, that's right," Tara admitted. "I had forgotten about my leg. Sometimes it gets stuck when I'm asleep, and that makes it hurt."

"I know, sweetheart," Mike said, his voice now heavy with emotion. "It's OK."

"It's been five years now since Tara's accident," I mused." It's hard to believe she was as small as Christa when it happened. She's getting so heavy; I wonder how much longer we'll be able to carry her. Oh well, we'll worry about that when the time comes. I'm sure God will show us a way."

As I lifted my head off the pillow, a wave of nausea washed over me, and I sank wearily back under the covers. "Morning sickness," I moaned. "And it's only just beginning. I wonder how many months of this I have to look forward to."

I still could hardly believe I was pregnant again. Right up until the last minute I had hoped it was something else. But yesterday Dr. Akrawi had confirmed my suspicions. "You are going to have a baby," he had beamed. "It will be due around April 5. Since you had such an extreme reaction to the anesthetic last time, we'd better take it natural all the way. I want you to take the Lamaze Natural Childbirth classes." I had gulped, forced a smile, and nodded.

A baby! I was actually going to have my fourth child. I didn't know whether to laugh or cry.

"O Lord," I prayed. "You know Mike and I hadn't planned to have any more children. To us, this is an accident. But I know you never make mistakes. You planned this baby for us, and I thank you for it. I know your gifts are always good. Lord, I am dedicating this baby to you right now. Please use this child in any way you desire, to bring glory to yourself. Thank you for giving to me the wonderful blessing of a new life. And please—somehow—help me get through this pregnancy!"

All the way home in the car, I alternated between elation and despair.

"Dear Lord—a baby! Oh, you know how I love babies! I wonder if it will be a boy or a girl! I love little girls, but a boy would round out our family so nicely. I'm glad I don't have to choose. We'll have to pick names—what fun! And I can again decorate a nursery—I love to do that! I wonder what the baby will look like. Will he or she be blonde like Christa? Or brunette like Tara? Or maybe have light brown hair like Mark? A redhead might be fun—my grandmother has red hair. O Lord, a soft, sweet, cuddly, warm, precious baby! I can hardly wait to hold it in my arms!"

But sandwiched in between all the happy, excited thoughts came the negative ones, just as fast and just as furious. "But, Lord," I moaned. "I'm not as young as I used to be. At thirty-one, I'm not sure I want to go through another pregnancy. And my pregnancies are so miserable! All that nausea and indigestion! And getting so big and fat and uncomfortable! And not being able to tie my shoes or roll over in bed at night! And swollen ankles! Not to mention the total exhaustion. Lord, don't you remember what a busy person I am? How can I possibly take time out of my already full schedule to have a baby? I don't get everything done even now! Whatever am I going to do? How will I find time to take care of a baby when it arrives?

"Mark is hyperactive. Remember, Lord? And Tara is completely helpless. How will I be able to lift her and take care of her and give her the hours of therapy she needs every day? I know I managed during my last pregnancy. But I was three years younger, and Tara was three years lighter. She's grown a lot since then. She weighs fifty pounds, Lord! And I'm only 5 foot 3. Have you forgotten? And what about Christa? She's only two years old. Haven't you heard of the Terrible Twos?

"What are my friends going to say? What are our parents going to say? How can I possibly explain another unplanned pregnancy?

"And Lord, what if the baby's not all right?

It will be, Lord. Won't it? Won't it? It has to be!"

From the depths of my being came the still, small voice of God. "Be still, and know that I am God," it seemed to say. "Don't you trust me? Haven't I always taken care of you? Haven't I always supplied your every need? Have you forgotten how much I love you?"

And instantly two verses from Scripture flashed into my consciousness. "And we know that God causes all things to work together for good to those who love God, to those who are called according to His purpose" (Romans 8:28). And, "My God shall supply all your needs according to His riches in glory in Christ Jesus" (Philippians 4:19).*

"God, my Father. Forgive me. It is I who have forgotten."

Why is it, I wonder, that when faced with a crisis, my immediate reaction is that God must have fallen off his throne and is no longer ruling the universe? I'm *sure* he has forgotten all about me and the plan he has for my life. I fuss and I fume and I worry, until God gently nudges me. "Donna," I can hear him say. "Remember me? I'm still in charge here." He so patiently reminds me of all he has done for me in the past, and so lovingly promises to see me through each and every problem. O God! You are so good!

Later that afternoon, Mike and I had worked up our courage and decided to call our parents. My mother, who loves each of our children dearly, but who vehemently disapproved of the timing of each one, was first. We called her at

*All references are from the *New American Standard Bible.*

her home in Bellaire, Texas. A stunned silence greeted our news. When she had recovered her voice, mother said carefully, "You know, I was so upset about your having Christa. I just didn't see how you could ever manage it, and it seemed like a real tragedy. But she is such a dear little girl, and she has been such a wonderful blessing to your family. I'm sure this new baby will be just as wonderful. Besides," she chuckled, "I've been wanting another grandson."

"Lord, I worried for nothing, didn't I? Do you think I will ever learn?"

Three years earlier, when Mike had told his parents I was expecting Christa, his mother's comment had been, "How could you do that to Donna? That poor little thing! How will she ever manage?" I think Mike approached this phone call with considerable trepidation. It seems that no matter how old we get, we hate to displease our parents.

We dialed Saratoga in northern California, and Mike explained the situation to his mother. Mike is the youngest of four children and was also unplanned.

"You know, Michael," his mother replied, "you were a surprise package, too; but we're awfully glad we had you. Just think," she went on, "we might have missed having you for our son. You have our blessings for your baby. May it grow up to be as fine as you."

The next people to be notified were those friends who were closely involved with Tara's therapy. For four years, we had had Tara on a program of neurological rehabilitation under the guidance of The Institutes for the

Achievement of Human Potential, in Philadelphia. As their director Glenn Doman puts it, "That's an awfully presumptuous name. Its only justification is that we mean to do exactly what it says."

Tara, who suffered massive damage to the mobility area of her brain at the age of two, had spent the past five years struggling to overcome the tremendous handicaps with which she had been left. And I had struggled right along with her.

Hour after hour, day after day, and year after year, I had encouraged, cajoled, and prodded Tara in her unceasing therapy. Eight hours a day, seven days a week, we had worked for so long. I had long since forgotten what it was like to lead a normal life. My whole existence was built around Tara and her therapy schedule. Someday, we hoped, Tara would be well again.

Tara's program, popularly called patterning, required a large corps of volunteer workers to perform. We usually had around 100 regular helpers coming in and out of the house each week. Many of them had been helping us since shortly after Tara's accident five years earlier. They had been through thick and thin with us, and still they came for an hour apiece each week to help move Tara's rigid limbs through her therapy program. I love these dedicated women, and I hated to have to tell them I was pregnant again. Soon I would be unable to do the more rigorous physical portions of Tara's therapy. And I knew that meant more work for the rest of her patterning team.

We use the team captain system for Tara's

volunteer schedule. For the five weekdays, one woman is in charge of each day. She is responsible for seeing that all the working hours on her day are filled with helpers, whom we call patterners. It was to these five wonderful women that I went with the news of my upcoming blessed event.

To my delight, not one negative word was expressed. "How wonderful," they all bubbled as one. "We're sure you're going to have a boy. God is going to round out your family!" They quickly swept away all my doubts about Tara's patterning schedules with admonitions that I was not to worry. They would take care of everything. Point by point, God was meeting and ministering to my needs.

A year earlier, we had met a most unusual young man. Terry Patané, at twenty-one, had been a very cynical, confused individual. He was a student majoring in biology at a nearby college, an admitted agnostic who didn't really know who he was or where he was going. All he really knew was that he was lonely and unhappy, that his life had no purpose. His entire life had always revolved around himself, and he had always prided himself on his ability to hide his true emotions and to remain totally uninvolved with anyone or anything. And if there was one thing he really didn't like, it was children. The less contact he had with them, the better!

Normally Terry read mostly books dealing with science. To this day, he can't explain why he had ever wanted to read the book *Tara*. A story about a brain-injured little girl?

Nothing could have been further from his interests! However, as he read the book he became so touched and so involved with the story that he could only read one chapter a day. He needed time in between to think.

During this time, he was filled with a burning desire to meet this little girl named Tara. He wanted to help her with her therapy; he wanted to become friends with her parents. And so it was that this shy, introverted young man knocked hesitantly at my front door one hot September day, thus beginning a warm and wonderful friendship. But more importantly, it was the start of a complete transformation in Terry's life.

Terry was anxious to do anything he could to help Tara. He patterned, he baby-sat, he built therapy equipment. He read her stories, he took her for walks. And every time he came over, I looked for opportunities to tell him about my Jesus. I just had to let him know that God was for real, and that God loved him. I wanted him to know that he didn't have to be lonely anymore.

His association with Tara had such a profound influence on Terry's life that he wrote a beautiful prayer to express his feelings and mounted it, together with a photograph he had taken of Tara, in a lovely frame.

PRAYER FOR TARA

While cradled within God's mighty hands, this fragile, beautiful child has sparked the dormant embers of our hearts, into flames of eternal love and everlasting faith. Within a few, courageous

years, she has become the foundation in a magnificent monument to the power and glory of God's eternal purpose!

Now, while I was pregnant, Terry was more helpful than ever. "You look so tired today, Donna," he would say. "You go in and nap this afternoon. I'll take your place in Tara's patterns." And I would gratefully, if not gracefully, waddle down the hall and curl up in bed to get more of the sleep of which I never seemed to have enough.

At times when I was feeling very discouraged about having another baby, God gave me some wonderful verses of Scripture to see me through. One of my favorites is this one from Psalms: "Behold, children are a gift of the Lord; the fruit of the womb is a reward. Like arrows in the hand of a warrior, so are the children of one's youth. How blessed is the man whose quiver is full of them."

Today, with everyone worrying about overpopulation, people tend to view multiple children as anything but gifts from God. And I guess more of this current philosophy had rubbed off on me than I had realized. But as I prayed and studied the Scriptures, I came to see that nowhere in the Bible is a baby greeted with anything but the greatest of joy. Children are one of the most wonderful gifts God gives us here on this earth. And having generously given me three, he was blessing me with yet a fourth. It should be an occasion for great rejoicing!

One Sunday morning, I woke up quite early. It was so quiet and peaceful in the house, and

I felt so serene and so close to God. I began praying for my family and for each one of my children. And then I asked, "Lord, will you give me a message from your Word today?"

I opened up the Bible expectantly, and it fell open to the book of Jeremiah. I had read Jeremiah when I read through the Old Testament several years earlier, but I had never studied it and didn't really know what in particular it contained. My thumb was resting on Jeremiah 1:4, 5, so it was to these verses that I directed my attention. As I read them, a shiver ran down my spine, and I felt the presence of the Holy Spirit in a very special way.

"Now the word of the Lord came to me saying, 'Before I formed you in the womb I knew you, and before you were born I consecrated you; I have appointed you a prophet to the nations.' "

I felt my swollen abdomen, and the baby within me was kicking and squirming. "Lord," I whispered in awe, "what does it mean?" I felt such an assurance that I would have a son, and that he would be a great man of God.

"Dearest Lord," I said, "only time will tell if this is indeed a revelation from you. But you know how much I would love to have a son who would eventually enter the ministry. Is this what you are telling me?" I felt peace washing over and over me. It was as if God were holding my baby and me and cradling us in his great arms of love. How grateful I would be for this assurance in the months to come.

CHAPTER TWO
Shannon Michael

I was lying flat on my back on the examining table, and Dr. Akrawi was measuring the size of my baby. "That's an awfully big baby for seven months," he said, scratching his head. "It's breech, too. Let's hope it turns; if not, we'll have to take it caesarean."

"Oh no," I groaned inwardly. "Caesareans are so expensive, and we don't have maternity insurance. They aren't quite as safe as normal deliveries, either," I worried, "and I'm not supposed to have anesthetic. And they take longer to recuperate from. I'm too busy for a long recuperation."

"Lord! Help!"

Oh, how I prayed. And I asked all my friends to pray, too. Sure enough, for one whole day my little one wiggled and squirmed, turning itself around. I could hardly wait for my next appointment. I was sure Dr. Akrawi would confirm that the baby was in the right position.

During my next visit, the doctor looked thoughtful as he listened for the baby's heartbeat through his stethoscope. I always enjoyed this, because the heartbeat was picked up on a sound unit, and I could hear it, too.

"You know," Dr. Akrawi smiled and said, "I think you may have twins in there."

"Twins?" I gasped. "O Lord," I said silently, "that's too much of a good thing. You know I don't have time to take care of twins."

I was scheduled for ultrasound pictures the next day. These are special sound-wave pictures taken with a giant camera similar to an instant-developing camera, and are safer for mother and baby than X-rays are. I could hardly sleep that night, I was so excited. In my mind, I kept going over and over how I could care for two babies and how I could fit two cribs into the tiny nursery.

We had moved Tara in with Christa and were turning Tara's small bedroom into a place for the new baby. At that moment, it looked like a disaster area. Terry was building me a diaper changing area in the closet, and the room was full of boards and tools. The walls were splotchy where half of Tara's yellow and white flowered wallpaper had been torn off. Rolls of yellow, blue, and green animal paper more suitable for a baby's room were stacked in a corner. The baby, or babies, were due in six weeks. I wondered if the room would ever be ready for them.

The hour for my appointment finally came,

and Mike and I were both on needles and pins. It was so exciting to think of having twins, but we both knew how much work two babies could be. How thankful we were that we could turn the whole problem over to God without the slightest doubt that he knew what was best for us.

After I spent an hour lying in positions I would previously have declared impossible for a very pregnant woman to assume, the lab technician was able to tell me with certainty that I was carrying only one baby. I couldn't decide whether to be happy or sad, so I settled for relieved—very relieved!

"That's a big baby you've got there, Mrs. Nason," the technician said with a smile. "If you carry it to term, it should weigh over ten pounds. It's seven-and-a-half pounds now. I don't see how you could go more than two more weeks before delivery."

I walked out of the office in a daze, clutching the pictures he had given me of my baby. "It's not every baby who is photographed before it is born," I thought. But on a deeper level, my mind was literally racing. "Two weeks! I'll never be ready!"

Three weeks later, during the night of March 10, I began to have some regular contractions, about twenty minutes apart. I could sleep in between them, but each time I had one, it woke me up. However, once morning came and I got up and began caring for the children, the contractions stopped.

"I guess it's just more false labor," I told Mike as he left for work. "Maybe so," he answered, "but why don't you notify the doctor just in case."

I did call the doctor, but he wasn't in his office that morning. The nurse said for me to call back if there were any further developments, but nothing else happened all day. I had a busy day scheduled for myself, ending with four hours of patterning Tara in the afternoon.

But when Terry arrived, he was emphatic. "Oh no, you don't," he commanded. "You'd better stay in bed all day and rest. I'll take care of everything for you." How luxurious I felt with a whole day to spend resting and reading!

Late in the afternoon, the nurse called to check on me. "I'd feel better if the doctor took a look at you before he went home tonight," she said. "Why don't you come on down now?"

Thank God for conscientious nurses and good friends who make you rest whether you want to or not.

Upon examination, the doctor found that my labor had indeed begun the night before and that the necessary dilation was already half completed. He noted, as I knew from previous experience, that when the contractions started again, it wouldn't take long.

"I don't want you having this baby in the car on the way to the hospital," he said sternly. "I know you feel fine now, but I want you to go on over and check in at the hospital."

"You mean it's really going to be born? Now?" I asked, excitement mounting in my voice. I had waited nearly nine months, but now I didn't think I could wait another minute.

I rushed home, called Mike to come home early from work, and put last-minute items in my suitcase. Terry would stay with the children, as I had previously arranged. I was so thankful to be leaving them in his capable hands.

They were each so excited that Mommy was finally going to have her baby. Tara and Christa were both screaming in delight, and Mark's smile went from ear to ear. How tenderly I kissed each one of them good-bye, telling them about the days each of them had been born.

Mike and I got to the hospital, and I was put in a labor room. We watched television for several hours, and finally the contractions began again. This time there was no doubt. By their intensity, I knew they were the real thing. I worked hard, concentrating on my breathing techniques learned in natural childbirth class.

In a matter of minutes, first stage labor was over and I was being wheeled into the delivery room. "My baby is almost here!" I wanted to shout for joy.

With Mike's help, I began pushing it out. Shortly the head appeared. "It's a blond," the doctor shouted. "Just a few more pushes and you'll have it made."

But the baby's shoulders were larger than its head, and they were in an odd position. Try as I might, I couldn't push them out. The big clock on the wall ticked the minutes off slowly, and still I struggled.

"Push—push—push," chanted the doctor, the nurse, and Mike in unison. I worked my body harder than I ever thought it could possibly work, my muscles tensed and throbbing. The pain, with no anesthetic, was intense. But that didn't matter. I had to get my baby out!

"If you don't deliver it within the next few minutes," the doctor urged, "it will die."

"Lord Jesus," I begged, "please help me push this baby out!" And suddenly it slipped out into Dr. Akrawi's hands.

"Here's your little football player," he shouted joyfully. "Look at the shoulders on that boy. He's huge!"

I grinned up at Mike. "A little blond boy," I whispered. I looked at the baby's little face, and it was all black and blue from bruising it had received during delivery. It had been harder on him than it had been on me, I realized. I wanted to just gather him up in my arms and take care of him.

The doctor was working feverishly over him, because he hadn't cried or moved at all. He administered oxygen to him as he worked, and finally the baby let out a tiny, weak cry. We all heaved a sigh of relief.

I watched the doctor give him his apgar test. This I was most interested in, because it can sometimes reveal brain damage in infants. I could see that the baby was not responding well at all and I bit my lips as he lay there listlessly. In an apgar test, ten is the highest score and anything under five is cause for concern. My baby scored four.

Dr. Akrawi didn't seem too concerned, though. "He's just come through such a traumatic delivery," he explained. "In all my years of delivering babies, that's the worst shoulder delivery I've ever seen. Another minute and we would have lost him for sure. And don't forget, he is three weeks premature, even if he does weigh eight pounds twelve-and-a-half ounces." He shook his head. "He was too big for you. I should have taken him caesarean. But he should do all right. Don't worry."

I was taken into a room and deposited in a bed. Every muscle in my body was shaking from the intense workout I had given it. Mike was holding my hand and stroking my hair. "We have our Shannon Michael," he said happily.

"I knew it would be a boy," I said thoughtfully. "I wonder what the Lord has planned for him. Something special, I think."

Soon I was left alone in the darkness of my room. I was exhausted, but so elated that sleep was a long time in coming. I just lay there in a kind of dreamy state, not quite asleep, but not fully awake either. Shannon had been born at half past midnight; it must surely be around 2 A.M. by now, I thought. Occasionally I could hear the nurses' soft-soled shoes glide down the hall, but otherwise all was still and quiet.

My door was half open, and my room was across from the nurses' station. The sound of a telephone being dialed broke the silence and roused me somewhat. Then I heard a nurse's muffled voice.

"We need a chest X-ray in the nursery right away," she said. "It's a newborn, and he's not breathing."

I was fully awake in a flash. "That's my

baby. I know it is. My baby isn't breathing." I was immediately encompassed in a helpless, smothering fear. It traveled up from the tips of my toes and choked in my throat.

Then I thought, "Oh, Donna, you're just being silly. There are several babies in the nursery. It's probably someone else's baby."

"What are you talking about?" I interrupted my own monologue. "Do you want someone else's baby to die? What a terrible thing to wish on someone else. Better for you to take the sorrow than to put it off on others."

And then that small voice I know and love so well took over. "It doesn't matter whose baby it is. It needs your prayers. If it's your baby, they'll tell you soon enough."

So I lay there in the darkness praying. I prayed for a tiny baby to live. I prayed God would give wisdom to the doctors working on it. I prayed that God would give strength to the parents of the baby.

"Dear Lord, please let that baby live. No matter whose baby it is, please let it live," I prayed over and over again, as tears stung my eyes and made rivulets down my cheeks.

I looked up and saw that my door had been shut while I was praying, but it was opening now. A nurse came in and gave me a pill.

"What's this for?" I asked suspiciously.

"Oh, it's just something to make you feel better," she replied with a smile.

"A likely story," I said to myself as the door closed, leaving me in darkness once more. I was sure the pill had something to do with the baby that wasn't breathing.

I resumed my prayer vigil, wondering what was happening down the hall in the nursery. I felt God's presence so strongly in the room; I knew he was there with me. I felt as though I were lying in his arms and he was rocking me to sleep.

"I love you, Donna," he seemed to say. "Don't worry. I'll see you through this too."

It seemed that I had just gotten to sleep when the door opened again. I blinked against the brightness of the light as it was turned on and looked up to see who my visitor was this time.

I was surprised to see Mike and realized he was not alone. Our pediatrician, Dr. Shannon, was with him. They both looked haggard and sorrow was written on every line of their faces.

"It was my baby," I thought to myself.

Mike cleared his throat. "He looks so tired and so sad," I thought.

"Donna," he began, "there's trouble with the baby."

"O Lord," I prayed. "How it hurts him to tell me. Please help it not to hurt so much."

"I know," I blurted out to Mike. "I know. But don't worry; I feel at peace about it. I know the Lord is with me."

And Mike and Dr. Shannon began to tell the whole story. At last I knew what had been happening in the nursery. A nurse had walked past the baby's bed around 2 A.M. and noticed that he was blue. Upon checking, she saw that he was not breathing. She had no way of knowing how long he had been in respiratory arrest.

She called in Dr. Shannon, waking him out of a sound sleep. He had dressed and driven over to the hospital, which was only a few minutes away. Even so, it took him around fifteen minutes to get there, and the baby still was not breathing when he arrived. We know Shannon was without proper oxygen to his brain for at least twenty minutes. Normally, permanent brain damage can result after only five minutes.

Dr. Shannon explained that the baby had turned black by the time he arrived, and he had ordered a chest X-ray to determine the origin of the problem. It was discovered that the baby had broken his collarbone during delivery, and this had punctured his lung. The remaining lung had struggled along as well as it could, but had eventually collapsed. It was at this time that the respiratory arrest had occurred.

Dr. Shannon had administered oxygen, reinflated the lung, inserted an umbilical catheter and endotracheal tube, and put the baby on a respirator. The baby was in very critical condition, much too critical to be cared for there at Mission Community Hospital.

Thirty miles away, he explained, was Orange County Medical Center, which had one of the best Neo-Natal Intensive Care Units in the country. He had sent for a team from their unit to transport the baby to Orange County. They had already arrived and were working with him.

Dr. Shannon's eyes clouded. "I'm no hero," he said plainly. "But your baby is alive. At best, he has only a small chance to live through this. If he does, only time will tell how much brain damage he will have. He is already posturing, making strange movements which indicate brain damage. I just could hardly believe it when I realized he was your baby. With Tara and all—it's too much!"

Just then another doctor dressed all in white came into the room, pulling down his mask around his neck so he could speak. "Mr. and Mrs. Nason, I'm Dr. Fletcher from Orange County Medical Center. I came down with two nurses from Neo-Natal, and we've been working on your baby. He is stable now, and we're ready to move him.

"He's a very sick little boy, but we'll do our best for him. He was without oxygen for a long time. You must realize his chances for brain damage are very high. We have him in a special isolette to create a perfect environment for him. It has just the right temperature, and we can control the percentage of oxygen in the air. We'd like you to see him before we take him away."

"I don't want to!" But the words died in my throat. Two nurses wheeled in a large isolette, totally enclosed in clear plastic. On another mobile stand came a heart monitoring device, beeping its message in green lights across the screen. Wires led from it into the isolette and were taped to the chest of its tiny occupant.

I caught my breath at the sight of him. My baby. The one I had carried inside me for nine months, who was so much a part of me. There were the little hands and feet whose jabs and pokes I knew so well.

He looked so unreal, like a little baby from

outer space. Human, but not quite. When his lung had collapsed, the air in it had escaped and gone under his skin. This had puffed up his chest, neck, and head, and made them appear grotesque and huge and out of shape. His face and head were even more bruised than I had remembered, and in his mouth the tube from the respirator was inserted. I heard the familiar swish of the machine as it forced the tiny chest up and down. Breathe—breathe—breathe, little baby, it seemed to say. His little body seemed to be covered with tubes and wires.

"Mrs. Nason," the doctor went on, "we'd like you to touch your baby. Just slip your hand through the porthole there on the side of the isolette."

He looked so tiny and fragile lying there. I was afraid. But I gingerly put my hand through the now-opened port and felt the soft, velvety skin. Afterward, Mike did the same. His eyes were swimming with tears, but I couldn't let myself lose control. Not yet.

Mike and Dr. Shannon followed the baby out to the waiting ambulance; they saw the nurses retract the legs of the isolette and slide it onto the floor of the ambulance and close the door, and then watched it race away with beacons of red lights in the night sky.

Mike felt a hand on his shoulder and turned around to see a policeman standing there. "Come on in," he said. "I'll buy you a cup of coffee."

CHAPTER THREE
A Tiny Golden Heartbeat

In my room, I lay in bed trying to sort out my thoughts.

"God! Why? Why again? Why brain damage? Lord, if he's going to be brain-damaged, please take him now. I simply can't handle another brain-injured child. I'm not strong enough. There's not enough time. There's not enough money.

"Dear God, why does it have to hurt so bad?"

I wondered how it would feel to go home to an empty nursery. Then I thought about the babies who would soon be brought in to their mothers to be fed. How can I stand it? How can I bear to watch the other mothers with their babies? I've got to get out of this place!

In my mind, I pictured all the bizarre forms brain damage can take, wondering which kind my baby Shannon might have. "If I could choose," I wondered, "which kind would I pick for him? Aphasia? Retardation? Autism? Cerebral palsy? No! No! No! A thousand times no! I don't want my baby to have any kind of brain damage! Well, God," I thought ironically, "if there had to be a brain-injured baby born at Mission Community Hospital on March 12, I'm sure that of all the mothers here I'm the one best qualified to care for it."

Daylight came; breakfast was served. Then came the moment I had been waiting for. My shower, with lots of noisy hot water and plenty of privacy. At last I could really cry, loud and long and hard. I was reminded of the Bible verse:

A voice was heard in Ramah,
Weeping and great mourning,
Rachel weeping for her children;
And she refused to be comforted,
Because they were no more. (Matthew 2:18).

And I thought of all the mothers who have lost babies over all the centuries, and the noise of their crying became as a great din in my ears.

"I am not the only one to go through this," I reminded myself. "I am not the first and I won't be the last. And I do not have to suffer alone. There is one who suffered much for me. My Lord Jesus will see me through this heartbreak too. I know he will; he has never let me down yet. I have his promises as revealed in the Bible, and I also have his promise which he gave directly to me. And," I reminded myself, "God never breaks his promises."

For an instant, I was tempted to be bitter against God for letting this happen. After all, how much can one person take? How many brain-injured children is it fair to give to one mother? How much heartache? How much sorrow? But I knew, even as the thought occurred to me, that I could never blame God or rail against him.

I stayed in that shower a long time, crying and praying to God. Finally, out of sheer exhaustion, I gave up.

"Shannon is your baby, Lord. I didn't even want him in the first place, but you gave him to me out of your great love. He is a love gift. In my will, I am saying I will not worry about him anymore. Now, I know it may take a while for my emotions to catch on to the idea. But with your help, I know they will. I know you have a wonderful plan for Shannon's life. I'm going to trust you for that plan. I'm going to claim his healing. I know you have the power to heal him, and I believe you want to and that you will make Shannon perfectly well. But, Lord, if I am mistaken, if your plan for Shannon does not include his healing, that also will I accept. How can I want my will over yours, when I know that you know better than I do what is best for me?"

Then I dried my tears and went back to my room. I was still a lonely young mother in a maternity ward without a baby. A dark, ominous cloud still hung over the future of Shannon Michael Nason. Outwardly, all the circumstances were still the same. It was I who was different. I had turned my problem over to

God, and I knew he would handle it in the best way possible.

Mike was there. How I thanked God for the quiet strength of my husband. He expected the best from me, and I gave him my best. The best smile I could muster, the best conversation I could think of.

He had called my mother, and she would be flying into Los Angeles in the afternoon. Mike's secretary and her husband, Marge and Phil Kurz, would pick her up and bring her straight to the hospital.

Terry had notified the prayer chain at my beloved Presbyterian Church of the Master. They had been in constant prayer since 3 A.M. All the people at Hour of Power were praying too.

No, Mike had not told Tara and Christa that their baby brother was very sick. Only Mark knew; he was very sad, but seemed to be handling it well.

Terry was devastated. As a fairly new Christian, he just couldn't understand how God could have let such a tragedy happen to his "second" family. He had stayed up praying and crying all night, all the while hammering boards into place in the still uncompleted nursery. He told me later that sometime around daybreak he was completely filled to overflowing with God's love. He felt bathed in God's peace. It was his first experience with the supernatural power of the Holy Spirit, God's Comforter. It was an experience he will never forget.

It is so hard to know why the painful things

happen to us here on earth. Someone once said that life is like a patchwork quilt. Usually all we can see are the knots underneath; but God, looking down from above, sees the beautiful design he is creating. I like to think that Shannon added a fabric of beautiful color and design to my quilt.

The phone in my room began ringing, flowers started to arrive, and a steady stream of friends began to flow in and out. Each one carried the same message. "We love you. We care. We're sorry you are hurting. We're standing by you in prayer."

So often when a friend is facing a tragedy, our first thought is to stay away. "I don't know what to say. I might break down," are some of the excuses we are likely to use. But to have my friends around me to talk to, to know I had their support, meant so much to me.

Our community of Mission Viejo, with its 45,000 residents, seemed to take Shannon's problems on a very personal level. Most people had read our book *Tara* or had seen the many articles in local papers written about her. Even if they didn't know us personally, they felt we were their friends. In parking lots and grocery stores, the news of our baby's plight was spread. Friends and relatives around the country were called, and a great incense of prayer went up before the throne of God.

Mike is privileged to have one of the most wonderful bosses in the world. As executive producer of the Hour of Power television program, he has as his boss (and very special friend) Dr. Robert Schuller. World-famous

Christian leader and founder-pastor of the 8,000-member Garden Grove Community Church, Dr. Schuller is an unusually sensitive, loving man. In the years we have known him, he has become very close to our family.

Shannon's problems affected him very deeply. Mike and I discussed it, and we decided to ask Dr. Schuller to baptize our baby and to pray for his healing. Dr. Schuller and his dear wife Arvella met Mike at the hospital. Only parents of the babies are allowed in intensive care there, and at first the nurse didn't want to let Dr. Schuller in.

"I really am their pastor," Dr. Schuller insisted. "Look; here's my baptismal bowl," he quipped, holding up the silver bowl full of water he had brought.

Arvella watched through the glass wall as Mike and Dr. Schuller went in to take their places by the isolette. Dr. Schuller, garbed in a green hospital gown, with a mask over his face, gently put his big hand through the porthole and laid it tenderly on the tiny bruised head. "I baptize you in the name of the Father, and of the Son, and of the Holy Ghost," he whispered solemnly into the antiseptic air. And all was silence.

I was allowed to leave the hospital the very next morning, only thirty-three hours after Shannon was born. Mike drove me straight to Orange County Medical Center and pushed me up to Neo-Natal Intensive Care in a wheelchair.

What an amazing sight greeted me there! A whole room full of isolettes, a different nurse standing by each one. Each one had a heart-monitoring screen next to it, keeping a constant check on its tiny occupant. They were mostly all premature babies; I had never seen any so small. Little living souls, with arms and legs no bigger around than my index finger. Some weighed no more than a pound and a half and often just forgot to breathe. When this happened, a buzzer would sound and the nurse assigned to the baby would poke at it through its porthole to remind it to take a breath. "Breathe, little mouse," one nurse repeatedly admonished her diminutive charge. I was fascinated as I watched the love and care each wee one received.

My baby Shannon, so small and new, looked large when compared with the other babies in the room. I was so thankful to see that he was breathing on his own and no longer needed the respirator. He could take nothing by mouth and was undergoing continuous intravenous feeding. He was seriously jaundiced, his downy skin tinted a sickly yellow; so they had him under a special light aimed at reducing the billiruben count in his bloodstream. He was lying on his tummy, his legs drawn up underneath him, his bare bottom in the air.

I sank wearily into a chair near Shannon's isolette, and took a long, hard look at my baby. Did he look like any of the other children? He was so swollen and out of proportion, it was impossible to tell. I wondered if he would die before I could hold him, and my empty arms ached with longing.

During the drive home, Mike shared with me his hopes that God would heal our baby. "He's going to be all right, Donna. I just know he is." Then he added wistfully, "He's got to be."

Years earlier, we had wondered which would be the hardest to bear: to have a child brain-injured in an accident as Tara was or to have a baby brain-injured at birth. Even now, we couldn't decide. Only one thing was for certain. They both hurt! But through the pain, we were both acutely conscious of God's love for us. He was upholding us, giving us strength. We could both feel it, and it was very real!

At home, my reunion with Mark, Tara, and Christa was so special to me. How I loved these children God had given me, and how very much I needed them! Their bright eyes and constant chatter were a real balm for my aching heart.

As the days passed, Shannon continued to improve. He was allowed out of the isolette for brief periods. Joy of joys, I was able to hold him, feed him his bottle. The jaundice began to slowly reduce, and the swelling began its gradual decline. At the end of a week, he looked very decidedly human; and, equally important, he was acting very normally.

As a mother experienced in the actions of both normal and brain-injured babies, I observed Shannon very carefully. I could see nothing amiss. Even so, it was wonderfully reassuring when the resident pediatric neurologist examined him and gave him a clean bill of health. "But," he warned ominously, "you must realize that as Shannon grows and develops, symptoms of brain injury could become apparent. With oxygen loss such as he suffered . . ." He stopped and shook his head.

Mike and I smiled knowingly at each other. The doctors were all baffled over Shannon's progress. They couldn't understand how this tiny baby could be doing the impossible. But they were not reckoning with the miracle-working power of God. They kept expecting the ugly signs of brain damage to appear, but Mike and I knew in our hearts that a miracle had occurred. God in his mercy had looked down with compassion and touched a tiny bit of humanity with his great, healing love.

Months earlier, we had picked out a beautiful birth announcement with the form of a baby sketched in black ink. On it were inscribed the words which now seemed especially appropriate.

What a Miracle—
A tiny golden heartbeat,
All brand new.

CHAPTER FOUR
Sinners and Saints

When Shannon was eight days old, we were able to bring him home from the hospital. Mike wheeled me through the linoleumed corridors in a wheelchair, and I snuggled Shannon close in my arms. He was just a tiny bundle wrapped in yellow blankets, but oh how much that tiny bundle meant to me. I hadn't known my heart could contain so much joy!

I couldn't help but remember, though, the day almost six years earlier when we had wheeled another bundle dressed in yellow out of intensive care and through the halls of the hospital toward home. The contrast sliced at my heart like a knife, the pain only slightly dimmed with the passage of time.

It had been Tara, then only twenty-six months old, that we had brought home that day. Tara, who, of my four children, was by far the most intelligent, the most coordinated, the best dispositioned. Tara who, I had been certain, was the sweetest, the prettiest, the smartest, the most wonderful little girl in the whole world. Tara, who could neither see nor speak nor respond in any way. She had been just as lifeless as the hospital bed on which she lay.

On August 9, 1970, Tara had sustained a great trauma of unknown origin. Mike and I had been away on vacation, celebrating our seventh anniversary, and Tara and Mark were in the care of a friend. In a way which is still unknown to us, Tara fractured her skull and her left arm. The impact of the blow bounced her brain around inside her skull, seriously bruising it and creating a massive cerebral hemorrhage. This sent her spiraling into a coma, and there she lay for many, many days.

The sorrow of those days is still written on my heart, and as Mike pushed baby Shannon and me through the hospital doors into the warm spring sunshine, my mind was flooded with memories of that other homecoming day and of the feelings and events that were to forever change my destiny.

How does it feel to see that which you value above all things lying motionless in a hospital bed; not seeing, not hearing, not even breathing, save for the rhythmic pulse of the respirator forcing her chest up and down? It hurts. It hurts with a pain more exquisite than it is possible to describe. And all the while the anger and the inner turmoil mount.

The questions came so fast and so furious that I could barely keep track of them. What is this thing called life? What is it all about? If beautiful little two-year-old girls can be pitilessly reduced in seconds to blithering vegetables, then what's the use? How can a loving God let this happen? Maybe there isn't a God! Or if there is, maybe he doesn't care about us! Maybe it's all just a big game to him and human life means no more than that of an ant or a fly. Why am I here anyway? I didn't ask to be born and suffer like this! Why did I bring children into a world where promising young lives are wrecked and dreams are smashed beyond recognition? Why? Why? Why? Was there no one who cared or knew the answer?

Like Job of old, I ran forward to find God and he wasn't there. I looked to the left, but he was gone. I searched to the right, but all was emptiness. I turned backward, but he eluded me there also. "My God! My God! Where are you? What are you? Can I ever hope to find you? By what name are you called? If I call you, will you answer me? If you answer me, what will you say?"

Ask, and it shall be given to you; seek and you shall find; knock, and it shall be opened to you (Matthew 7:7).

Little did I know during those, the darkest days of my life, that I was embarking upon the most exciting, the most thrilling, the most fulfilling quest possible for any human being to pursue. I had no way of realizing the great joy such a search would bring me. At that time, I was certain of only one thing: the great uncertainty of life and the pain that it brings.

I remember standing in the small lounge for parents at Children's Hospital in Orange, California. The room was full of different family members, huddled in forlorn little groups, each one thinking his own private thoughts and asking his own private questions. It was very quiet except for the great sobs convulsing Mike's body as he sat with his head in his hands. Salty tears trickled through his fingers and splashed onto his lap. He looked up suddenly at the minister who had married us and who had come to console us while Tara's life lay in the balance. Mike's eyes opened wide and he gulped out one agonized word—"WHY?"

Rev. Bob Tourigney, in an uncharacteristic show of emotion, hit the palm of his left hand with his right fist—hard—and raised his voice to almost a yell as he spat out, "Sin! Man has sinned!" His outburst was so loud, so out of character, and so unexpected that Mike was silenced immediately. Every eye in the room was riveted on the tall man in the dark suit and white clerical collar, but he said no more. I guess he felt there was no more to be said.

Later that night, Mike and I lay in bed, our tears momentarily dried. We could feel the darkness, and stillness was a cloak that pressed close. We were both quiet and deep in thought. It was Mike who broke the silence. "Donna," he whispered softly, "what do you think Rev. Tourigney meant this afternoon?"

I thought for a long time. "You mean about

sin?" I asked. "I don't know. I just don't understand anything anymore."

"Neither do I," he sighed. "Good night."

I don't know how long I lay there in the darkness thinking about sin. What is sin anyway? Do I sin? Did Tara sin? Is she hurt because of my sin? Because of her own sin?

I didn't find an answer either that night or in the days to follow. It was a haunting question that wove itself into the very warp and woof of my being. I had so many questions; I had so much to learn. Who knew the answers? Did anyone know?

In the months that followed, Tara gradually came out of her coma. It was a slow, heartbreaking process with many setbacks. But at least we had our little girl back home. It wasn't really my beautiful, laughing Tara that I tucked into that crib each night, but a stranger. The strangest stranger I had ever seen. A little girl who could neither see, nor move, nor speak. A little girl whose spirit was in such anguish that it cried out all day in the eerie sound her doctors called a "brain cry."

I wanted Tara to get better so badly, I was willing to try anything! I took her to a miracle healing service being given by Kathryn Kuhlman. Miss Kuhlman was talking about sin, and my ears perked up. The only trouble was, she didn't give a good definition of what sin really is. I knew that murder and adultery and stealing and things like that were sins. But I had never done things like that and neither had Tara.

Thus began a search that took me many

years. I decided to begin with the Bible and started at the beginning in the book of Genesis. I saw that God created a perfect world. He never intended little two-year-old girls to be the victims of massive brain damage. He never meant for mothers to cry themselves to sleep night after night in anguish for their children.

God created a perfect world to be enjoyed and loved. A world where there would be no disease, no injury, no tears, no heartaches. God created beautiful trees and flowers, animals to roam the land and fish to glide in the sea. Each one of these served an ecological purpose in the balance of nature.

God is a God of balance and of order. Did he not invent all the natural laws of the universe and put them into working order? God is the greatest scientist of all time! And so God set up the intricate chain of life, with each plant and animal dependent upon the next for its ultimate survival. He made each link in the chain vital and important, no matter how unimportant it may seem.

And then God did something different. He created something that had no ecological significance whatsoever. He breathed life into a creature that had no place in the balance of nature. Mankind!

Why did God, who had taken such great care to establish a balance of nature, who had given every creation an ecological purpose, create man with no place in this grand design? The Bible answered this question for me. God created man in his own image and for the express purpose of glorifying himself. Man's only reason for existence is to glorify God.

But what does it mean to glorify God? My favorite Bible teacher, Wes Harty, says it means to reflect God's character and nature. So God created Adam and Eve perfect, with a free will and with the ability to reflect his own character and nature.

As I continued my study, I realized that God told Adam and Eve there was only one thing they couldn't do. They couldn't eat the fruit of one particular tree in the garden.

Now why, I wondered, did he pick out something like that? And I suppose he could have picked out nearly anything as the one rule he gave to them. God had provided them with plenty of fruit and other good things to eat. They certainly weren't going hungry! And yet they disobeyed and ate the forbidden fruit! And the Bible calls their disobedience sin. Does that mean that anytime I disobey God, I am sinning? I'm afraid it does.

How many times did Adam and Eve have to disobey God before they were sinners? Just once! As Ken Poure, one of the directors of Hume Lake Christian Camp in California, says, "How many times do you have to tell a little white lie before you are a liar?" And he answers his own question, "Just once!"

"So," I thought, "that's what sin is, and I am a sinner." I had never thought of myself as a sinner before, and the revelation was rather a shock for me. "Oh," I rationalized to myself, "but I'm not a bad sinner. I mean I don't ever do anything really terrible. I'm just a little sinner." But I couldn't help but notice that God doesn't seem to make a distinction between so-called big sin and little sin. After all, Adam and

Eve lost their home in the Garden of Eden just for eating one piece of fruit. To God, sin is sin.

The Bible says in Romans 3:23, "For all have sinned and fall short of the glory of God." One day in a Bible study, Wes Harty explained that to fall short means to miss the mark. It means that every human being that has ever lived, beginning with Adam, has not been able to meet God's standard of perfection. And to not meet God's perfect standard means sin, because we were created to reflect God's perfection and we are failing to do so.

But what has all this got to do with Tara? What does the fact that people sin have to do with the permanent marring of a little girl's life? I wondered. I read and I thought and I studied. I went to hear the so-called experts. I studied not only what the Bible has to say about this, but also what many of the ancient and modern philosophers have said regarding this confusing subject. However, I always kept coming back to the Bible. It seemed to make such good sense to me.

At one time we were considering enrollment for Mark in a private school. I took Mark with me to Maranatha Academy, a Christian school associated with Calvary Chapel, a church with a special approach to youth ministry. While we eventually decided to keep Mark in public school, I was very impressed by Maranatha Academy and its staff. One thing the principal said really meant a lot to me. He looked very seriously at eight-year-old Mark and asked, "Have you read any love letters lately?"

Mark, who was thoroughly embarrassed by

the whole ordeal anyway, shook his head and concentrated his gaze on a hole in the toe of his tennis shoe. The principal continued, "The Bible is God's love letter to you. He wrote it because he loves you, and he wants you to know about him and the way he thinks and acts. He wants you to know the way he wants you to live. And he wants you to have the answers to all your questions. If you were the only person on earth, God would still have written the Bible just for you." Mark's big blue eyes got even bigger, and a smile turned up the corners of his mouth and wrinkled across his little freckled nose. "Really?"

And so, over the years, this is how I have come to see the Bible. It is God's love letter to me, and in it are the answers to all my questions. It only remains for me to ferret them out.

And so I continued my search in earnest. I just had to find an answer for human suffering in general and my family's own suffering in particular!

All around me, I see suffering. There is not one family that is not touched with pain and heartache at one time or another. Since I frequent rehabilitation centers for brain-injured children, I am particularly sensitive to this great area of sorrow. I have seen brain injury in all its forms and am personally well acquainted with the deep grief it brings. I have seen vital, popular young teenagers reduced to lonely misfits from brain injury as a result of traffic accidents. I have seen active toddlers sparkling with life reduced to children who lay year after year with unblinking eyes and unsmiling faces while their mothers fed them blended food through a tube in their stomachs.

Recently my mother called from Texas to tell me that my cousin, Buddy Henson, a fine young man of twenty-five, had fallen from a tree and broken his neck and died instantly. Among those grieving at his funeral was the young woman he was to have married shortly. Why, God? Why?

And again the answer comes. There is sin in the world. God made our world perfect, but when sin entered it, the perfection was marred. God is a God of order and of natural and spiritual laws. When sin entered the world, death and pain and sorrow and tears also entered. We are subject to both natural and spiritual law, and God does not often break his own laws.

Given certain circumstances, certain things will happen. If an apple comes loose from a tree, it will fall to the ground, because of God's law of gravity. This is a good law, because it keeps us and everything on our planet from flying away. But if a man loses his grip on a tree, he will fall too. And if he is up high enough and falls in just the right way, it will break his neck and sever his spinal cord. If the cord is severed high enough, it will kill the man. It is a natural law.

If a little two-year-old girl gets a blow of sufficient magnitude on her head, it will cause damage to her brain. This is simply a natural law.

"But, Lord!" I cried. "It's not fair! It's

immoral! It's unjust! I thought you were a just God!" How can a just God permit the death of a fine upstanding young man and yet leave murderers and perverts alive? How can he allow robbers to be healthy and strong, and yet let an innocent child be brain-damaged and crippled for life? Is this justice?

Even as I ask the question, the answer eludes me. The only thing of which I am certain is that in this life I will never fully understand. The Bible says in Romans 11:33:

Oh, the depth of the riches both of the wisdom and knowledge of God! How unsearchable are His judgments and unfathomable His ways!

There are some things that the finite mind is simply unable to comprehend.

But I have surely come to many conclusions about suffering. In the first place, we must realize that God loves both the sinner and the saint. I have trouble with that concept, and I think most people do. It's hard to love the unlovely. But God does—he can do it, because he is God.

In addition, God's whole view of life is completely different from ours. And why shouldn't it be? He is not limited by time and space. God is eternal, and he views human life from the perspective of eternity.

What is eternity? How can I ever even begin to understand it? How can I cope with a life where there is no time, no birth, and no death? I can possibly envision no ending. But no beginning? Have you ever wondered when and how God got started? I have; I've wondered and questioned and thought about it a lot. And I don't think I'll ever understand how a being can have always existed. And yet God has.

But imagine what a human lifespan must be to God. A wink of an eye? No, not even that long. And how shall it matter in view of eternity whether that span is two years or twenty-five years or 125 years?

"Yes, God, but it sure matters a lot to me! And that still leaves the problem of justice. The Bible says you are a just God, and I believe it. Yet where is the justice in this world?" I guess the real answer to that is that there is no justice in this world.

My Tara comes home from school and often asks, "Mom, can I go outside this afternoon in my wheelchair?"

"No, Tara. You know you have your therapy to do all afternoon."

"But I'm tired of therapy. I don't want to do it today. Why do I have to? It's not fair!"

What can I say? "Tara, at the age of two you deserved to be in a tragic accident and it's only fair that you be crippled for life and do therapy all afternoon every day"? Of course I can't say that! It's not true! Tara doesn't deserve the handicaps she has.

But I believe God is just. I always tell my children not to expect things to always be fair in this world. It is an imperfect world, marred and distorted by sin. But in eternity, justice will prevail. All things will be set straight, the scales of justice balanced. The lives we lead here will seem so small and insignificant, and God will kiss every tear away. I always tell

Tara, "There will be no wheelchairs and no therapy in heaven."

"Oh, Mommy," she says, " I can hardly wait. Do you think I will be going soon? I'm going to walk all the way to Jesus' house and sit in his lap and sing and sing. And you won't have to braid my hair anymore. I will do it all by myself." And her face is radiant in anticipation.

One day I came to God in prayer and asked, "How, Lord? How are you going to bring about justice in eternity? The Bible says that all have sinned and that sin brings death. Lord, that means me, doesn't it? I wish I could say that I'm perfect and sinless, but I'm not. And I know that no one knows that better than you.

"For you were watching me when I rebelled against my parents as a child. You knew me as a popular teenager more interested in my clothes and my looks and my boyfriends than in helping others. You were there when I stormed out of baby Mark's room and slammed his door and screamed 'I hate you!' to the empty walls out of sheer frustration at my inability to quell his crying. You heard me when I lied, when I said that unkind word. You know my innermost thoughts. You know I am often selfish and rebellious. You hear me when I say to myself, 'I want it *my* way! Right now!'

"O Lord! Have mercy on me, for I am a sinner!

"I may be able to hide my sins from the world, and I can even fool myself sometimes. But I can keep no secret hidden from you. You know it all!"

I felt like I wanted to run and hide

somewhere. But where? Where can I ever go to hide from God? I know that no matter how hard I try, no matter how good I strive to be, I can never come anywhere close to God's standard of perfection. I can never earn a pardon from death. I can never work my way to heaven.

What joy the day I learned that I didn't have to earn my own salvation! Jesus had taken my death sentence, and in him I was free! God had been calling me to himself all the time, patiently, tenderly, lovingly. He had painstakingly shown me his love so many times, in so many ways. How had I missed it? How had I failed to see God's great love for me?

He had called to me over and over again, "Donna, I love you! I love you! Don't you understand? I love you!"

"But, Lord," I had questioned, "how can you love me? I am nothing. Oh, I know I sometimes think I'm important. But I'm not really. Often I am even worse than nothing. How can you, the Creator of the universe, love me?"

"Donna," came the voice from deep within me, "I love you. I have always loved you. I love you just as you are. I love you in your loneliness, in your frustration. Yes, I love you even in your sin. That is why I sent my Son to die for you."

"For me, Lord? Did Jesus really die for me?" I was incredulous.

God showed me, without a shadow of doubt, that Christ died for me. I firmly believe that if I were the only person who ever lived on planet earth, Jesus would still have died just for me.

He loves me that much. And his great love takes in the whole world. It reaches out to every person, regardless of his circumstances, no matter how great or how small, and says, "I love you. I died for you. I want to be your friend. If you ask me to, I will come and live in your heart. I will forgive your sins. I promise I will never leave you nor forsake you. I will guide your life. I have a beautiful plan for you; did you know? When you are sad and lonely, I will be there to dry your tears. When you are happy, I will rejoice with you. There is nothing, no, nothing, greater than my love. My love has overcome the world, and it has already overcome every problem you will ever encounter. You can count on me. I never change. I will always speak the truth, and I never break my promises."

"God," I answered, "what can I say in response to such great love?" I did the only logical thing I could think of under the circumstances. I accepted the love God has for me. I invited Christ into my heart and asked him to live with me forever. It was a simple prayer, but I meant every word of it.

I expected emotional fireworks, tears, overflowing joy; but instead I received none of these things. Only God's voice saying, "Trust me, I have answered your prayer."

It was a beginning. The start of the most beautiful, the most wonderful relationship in the whole world. Where I would be today without my friend Jesus, only God knows. Lonely and afraid; empty. Who would guide me and direct my paths? Who would be the framework for the portrait of my life? Who would cry with me when I am sad? Who would sing with me in my joy? Everything that I am or will ever be, every strength that I possess, is inseparably linked to God, to the commitment I made to him that day, and to the great friendship that has followed.

"Thanks be to God for His indescribable gift!" (2 Corinthians 9:15).

CHAPTER FIVE
Write a Book? Who-Me?

As I was struggling to adjust to being the mother of a severely brain-injured little girl, I kept asking people, "Am I the only one this has ever happened to? Is Tara the only child in the world to be brain-injured in an accident like this? Surely someone has written a book on the subject."

But try as I might, I was unable to find any book to which I could relate. To my knowledge, at that time there were no books written about children who had been brain-injured in accidents. "Well," I confided to Mike one day, "if I ever live through this, I'm going to write my own book. Maybe someday it could help someone else whose child has been hurt."

The months went by, and I became weighted down by the sheer physical drudgery of caring for the two children. Tara had to be driven thirty miles each day to a rehabilitation center so she could receive physical therapy. In addition, I tried to give her three hours of therapy myself at home. She had to be fed and dressed and have her diapers changed. I was trying to toilet train her and to teach her to talk again. I would mutter to myself, "It's bad enough to have to toilet train a child once, but twice is ridiculous!" Not only that, but she couldn't sit up; so I had to hold her on her little potty seat so she wouldn't fall off onto the floor! Mark was a perfect study in perpetual motion. It would have kept two mothers busy just chasing after him alone. Gradually, as I fought just to keep body and soul together, my dream of writing a book faded away.

However, unknown to me, my dynamic husband had other ideas. Although he didn't speak of it, he never lost his dream that a book should be written about our Tara.

Mike is an extremely handsome young man. With his masculine, chiseled features and his smooth, dark brown hair and clear blue eyes, he looks like the models who smile at us from the pages of magazines. Add to that a quick wit, a keen business sense, and a real "salesman" personality, and you've got quite a combination!

Once he talked me into buying an Irish setter, which with our small unfenced yard and our community with strictly enforced leash laws, was like declaring open war on the dogcatcher. My mother had been amazed.

"How on earth did you ever let Mike talk you into that big dog?" she asked me one day.

"Mother," I replied, "if you were married to a super salesman like I am, you wouldn't ask!"

Before we were married, Mike had been quite honest in telling me of his great love for politics. "If I ever get the chance," he had said on more than one occasion, "I'm going to run for public office. At the very least, I intend to be involved in campaign work." Love is blind, as they say, and even though I had no interest in politics and certainly didn't want to be married to a politician, I dismissed his ambition as a late-adolescent dream. I figured he would never get far and would likely tire of it soon. I figured wrong.

At the time of Tara's accident, Mike was on a leave of absence from his job as a sales executive for a fireworks company and was working full time as a paid staff member in Senator George Murphy's campaign for reelection here in California.

That was followed by a three-month stint in helping Governor Reagan with his welfare reform program. In 1972, Mike was hard at work on the full-time staff of the Committee to Reelect President Nixon.

We were Christians by then, and I had a strong feeling that God had a better plan for Mike's life than politics. "Michael," I kept saying, "I don't know what it might be, but God can use a man with your talents. If you would work as hard for Jesus as you are working for the President, I think spectacular things could happen."

It was during this time that we had the privilege of meeting Dr. Robert Schuller and his wife, Arvella, at a dinner party. Dr. Schuller's Hour of Power television program, one of my favorites (which is actually a video tape of his Sunday morning service at Garden Grove Community Church), was being televised on six stations across the country at that time.

Dr. Schuller asked Mike about his occupation and interests, and Mike explained his love for politics, sales, public relations, and like subjects. To my surprise and delight, Dr. Schuller said, "We could use a man like you in our organization. Why don't you give me a call next week?" He handed Mike his business card.

Mike thought Dr. Schuller was just being polite, but I felt the offer was truly from God. "Maybe this is the job God has for you to do," I urged him. Mike began work for Dr. Schuller on a volunteer basis, putting his political knowledge to work in an effort to free Christian pastors imprisoned behind the Iron Curtain. The two men worked together on this project for several months and became close friends.

One morning Dr. Schuller, or Bob, as Mike now called him, asked Mike to come over and meet with him. On the way over in the car, Mike was thinking, "I bet he's going to offer me a job today." And he was right! Mike was asked to become Dr. Schuller's Executive Assistant.

God had been preparing our hearts for this important job change for months. "Michael," I bubbled, "it's the perfect place for you. I just knew the Lord had a spot for you in his full-time service!"

Two weeks later, Mike went in to tell Dr. Schuller he had decided to accept the position.

One of Dr. Schuller's favorite slogans is "It's not odd, it's God," meaning that coincidences are never really coincidences but are planned and carried out in the providence of God. What was about to take place that day certainly falls into that category.

Dr. Schuller has written eleven books over a period of fourteen years. In all that time, he has never had a publisher come to visit him in his office but once. That one time just happened to be the very next appointment after Mike's that eventful day.

"Since you'll be coming to work for me now," Dr. Schuller said to Mike, "why don't you stay over for my next appointment and meet the editor-in-chief of Hawthorn? They'll be publishing my next book."

Mike did stay, and as the meeting was drawing to a close Dr. Schuller mentioned to Mr. Heckleman, the editor, that we had a very special little girl and that he thought a book about her would make interesting reading. Dr. Schuller proceeded, in his own inimitable way, to tell a little of Tara's story.

Mr. Heckleman was impressed and set a date to talk more about the project. Mike wrote a short synopsis and took some pictures of Tara with him when he went to see Mr. Heckleman. The editor liked what he saw and asked us to send him a sample chapter. Mike was so excited when he got home that night. "They really want to make Tara's story into a book!" he exclaimed.

"Do they have someone in mind to ghostwrite it?" I asked.

"No," he replied. "They want us to send them

a sample of our writing, and then they'll tell us if we need one or not."

"Michael, do you mean we might have to write the book ourselves? We don't know how! When would we ever find the time?" I was horrified. Then he told me they wanted the sample chapter mailed within a week. The week in question just happened to be the week before the Fourth of July. Mike, who was finishing up his job as a fireworks' representative before starting with the Hour of Power, was as busy as Santa Claus on Christmas Eve.

Of necessity, it became my task to write the first chapter of *Tara*. "Lord," I prayed, "you know I like to write, and journalism was my major in college, but I sure enough don't know how to write a book. If you want me to write it, you'll have to give me a lot of help!"

Each time I sat down to write, I tried to empty my mind of my own thoughts. I prayed that God would write the book through me by the power of his Holy Spirit. And I asked one main thing—that the book *Tara* would glorify God.

I mailed the first chapter to Hawthorn, and within a few weeks I received a reply. My stomach was invaded by a horde of butterflies as I looked at that big, white, impressive envelope. I was afraid to open it. What would it say? For that matter, what did I want it to say?

Inside was a cover letter and a contract! The editors at Hawthorn had liked my sample chapter and wanted me to write the book. The contract stated I had four months in which to write it.

Four months in which to write a whole book!

How would I ever manage? Where should I start? From the beginning it was a family project. Mike and I mapped out the chapters; I wrote, he edited, I rewrote. Tara's wonderful patterners came and put her through her paces as I sat for hours at the kitchen table, pen in hand. Friends took baby Christa to their homes so I could have uninterrupted time to work.

Finally, just before Christmas of 1973, it was finished. As I held the final typed manuscript in my arms, I felt as though I'd just had a baby! So private and so personal was the book, I wondered how I could ever stand to let anyone read it!

In the months that followed, there were galleys to read and correct, and then the big day in August arrived, when I actually held in my hand the completed book. Tara's happy face was smiling from the cover, and Mike and I just couldn't help it; we cried for joy!

To think that the power of God had taken a lonely, confused family faced with a problem of enormous proportions and so molded and shaped their lives that their story could be a blessing to others! On human terms it was incomprehensible, but with God nothing is impossible!

We wanted to share our joy with our friends and decided to give a party. We invited everyone whose name appeared in *Tara*. Linda Payne, who had taken many of the photographs for *Tara,* helped me make hors d'oeuvres, and Sonia Scott, one of my team captains, baked and decorated a beautiful chocolate cake shaped like an open book.

We asked Dick Bush, pastor of my local

Presbyterian church, to come and offer a prayer dedicating *Tara* to the glory of God and asking that lives might be changed through it. Then we gave a book to each couple. It was amazing how fast the party broke up after copies of the book were handed out. Everyone wanted to run home and read it. The lamps were burning late in Mission Viejo that night!

The entire Nason family heaved a joint sigh of relief. Thank goodness, we thought, no more books to write. Now we can get back to business as usual. But is there really any such thing as "business as usual" when your family is as unusual as ours? I wondered!

CHAPTER SIX
Sickness and Health

In November of that year, Tara had to go back into the hospital for more tests on her bladder. She had fallen prey to a succession of bladder infections which we had been unable to halt. We had to know why! I admitted her the afternoon before and settled her in the pediatric ward. Her trembling legs and constant chatter told me she was frightened, but she wouldn't admit it—even to herself. She was working overtime to maintain her facade of bravery, and I couldn't help but gaze at her with pride.

At six Tara still looked like a little pixie. Her dark brown hair was so long she could sit on it. It was thick and shiny, and I loved to brush it until it glistened. Because she couldn't sit up very well, it was always falling in her face, so I usually braided it for her in an effort to keep it out of her eyes and mouth. Her eyes were getting darker. Some people thought they were brown, others said gray or hazel. Whatever the color, rimmed by her long black curly eyelashes, they were beautiful. A sprinkling of freckles dusted her rosy cheeks, and she wore as always her perpetual smile.

As I was unpacking her bag, the door opened and in burst a nurse in her white uniform. "Is this the Tara Nason who spent such a long time in Children's Hospital four years ago?" she asked breathlessly. "I'm Pat Moriarity. I was one of her nurses in intensive care! The memory of that child has haunted me ever since, and many's the time I have wondered how she was doing."

Nurse and patient were joyfully reunited, and three pairs of eyes were puddled with tears. Pat pried us with questions and praised God for every answer we gave. She stood open-mouthed in awe over Tara's incredible progress—her speech and her intelligence. "It's a miracle," she kept repeating blissfully.

She told us she was a Christian who had found Christ at Garden Grove Community Church. After she had cared for Tara, she had spent a wonderful year at L'Abri in Switzerland. Since that meeting, Pat has repeatedly endeared herself to our family, spending countless hours baby-sitting and taking our children on special excursions they would never otherwise have enjoyed.

Later that night, Dr. Schuller arrived to pray with Tara and to express his love for us. In that cold, impersonal hospital room, our hearts were warm and full of the love of God sent to us in the person of this dynamic man of faith who had taken time from his busy schedule to drive the thirty miles from his home to the hospital.

When visiting hours were over, Mike and I were torn about leaving Tara there alone. She still seemed so young and so helpless to stay all by herself. But nevertheless, rules are rules. We prayed with her and assured her that God loved her and that Jesus would be with her all night. Her legs were shaking and her elfin face was grave, but she didn't cry.

The next morning the tests went well. The urologist explained to us that the bladder problems Tara has are only another symptom of her brain damage. Tara's brain keeps all of her muscles stiff and rigid, including the ones in her bladder area. "It's something she's just going to have to live with," he said. Was there ever to be an end to the far-reaching effects of Tara's brain damage? I turned the question over and over in the private recesses of my consciousness.

Meanwhile, back in her room, Tara was dreadfully nauseated, as she always is following general anesthetic. Mike, Terry, and I took turns holding the basin, washing her pale little face, and changing her soiled gowns.

They let us take Tara home that evening before dinner, and it was a rather subdued little girl who snuggled gratefully between the frilly yellow sheets of her bed. With the amazing resiliency possessed only by the very young, Tara was back to her effervescent self within a day or so.

But Mark wasn't feeling well. He had started complaining of a headache on Monday, the day Tara entered the hospital. We had been so busy with Tara on Tuesday and Wednesday, we hadn't had a chance to keep a close watch on Mark. We had sent him to school each day, but Thursday afternoon the director called to say he had spent most of his time lying down in the nurse's office.

Thursday evening and night, the headache's intensity increased at an alarming rate. Mark's eyelids were leaden with pain, the listless blue of his eyes barely showing. He had no fever and no other symptoms. What could it be? Fear hammered at my heart.

We put him to bed early, but sleep wouldn't come. He moaned and cried out in pain, and all during the night we kept having to run downstairs to quiet him. Aspirin gave him no relief. In the early morning hours, as Mark again woke us with his crying, Mike's groggy voice said, "Didn't Mark have a terrible headache like this once before? What caused it that time?"

Through a blanket of sleep, my mind began searching its memory banks. Mark had suffered headaches like these before. But when? Then it hit me. "When he was five," I said. "It was when he had spinal meningitis. But it wasn't just headaches then; he also had terrible nausea and vomiting. Remember? This can't be the same thing. Besides, you can't get spinal meningitis twice. Can you?"

Just then Mark came bounding up the stairs screaming and vomiting. "I can't stand it! I can't stand it!" he shrieked as he fought to fit the words in between the violent heaving.

"Oh, no," I thought. "It can't be! It just can't be!" There was no going back to sleep now, so I sat up the rest of the night with Mark while he vomited almost constantly. His eyes were dull and sunken inside dark-rimmed sockets; he was so weak, he could barely lift his head off the pillow. "Lord," I called out wearily into the darkness, "what's wrong with him?"

At 7 A.M., I called and arranged to take Mark in to the doctor as soon as he arrived in his office at 9:00. I asked Tara's patterners to come a few minutes early and take care of Christa for me. All the while, Mark was vomiting and crying frantically, "I can't wait until 9:00! I'm too sick!"

He was too sick, but I didn't know what else to do. Mike had to go to work, Tara and Christa had to be fed and bathed and dressed. "Lord," I asked for the thousandth time, "why didn't you make me twins? Maybe then I could handle everything."

Our own doctor was out of the office that day. The doctor on call didn't know our family, but he knew a sick little boy when he saw one. His face was serious as he examined Mark.

I clenched my fists and dug my fingernails deep into the palms of my hands as I watched him give Mark what I knew was a neurological examination. "Has he received any blows to the head recently?" he asked.

I winced. "No." I was trying so hard not to let Mark see how scared I was.

The doctor called me aside. "I'm reasonably

certain this child has spinal meningitis," he said. "I want you to take him directly to the hospital. You can get his things from home later. I'm going to order a complete series of test."

"Jesus," I whispered, "not again, surely not again."

The medical center shares its parking lot with the hospital, and I couldn't see any parking places closer than the one I already had. Mark was too weak to walk, so I lifted up my nine-year-old son and carried him in my arms into the hospital. His condition was deteriorating rapidly, and I seriously questioned whether he would live.

As soon as Mark was settled in a room and had a nurse caring for him, I ran to the lobby to call Mike. When I told him the news, Mike said he felt as though an electric shock were going through him, and he began to cry. He had been in a meeting with Dr. Schuller at the time, and the two of them immediately left their work and headed south down the freeway toward Mission Viejo.

A quick call to my Friday team captain, Iris Bjorklund, assured me that Tara and nineteen-month-old Christa would be well taken care of. In fact, Iris took them both home with her that day and kept them for me all weekend.

Mark was deathly ill all day and quickly became dehydrated, so that intravenous feeding became necessary. I trotted back and forth down the hall by his bedside as they wheeled him around for his various tests and X-rays.

All during the day, the pastors from various

local churches came to see us. They had seen Mark's name on the hospital's patient list and had come by to pray. In total, he had five different pastors (one Baptist, two Presbyterians, and two Reformed Church ministers) lay hands on him and pray for his healing. I know God sent these valiant men of prayer to Mark just when he needed them the most.

Late that afternoon, three doctors came in to do a spinal tap. They warned us that they were certain it would reveal meningitis. Mike and I huddled in the parents' lounge and prayed and waited, our hearts numb with disbelief. It seemed an eternity, but at last they were through.

When they came in to speak with us, they admitted they were frankly puzzled. Mark's case presented classic meningitis symptoms, but the spinal fluid had been clear. None of the tests or X-rays revealed anything to explain the severity of Mark's illness. "We don't know what's wrong with him," they said. "We'll just have to wait and see what develops."

Mark was so ill that he just lay still in his bed, too weak even to speak most of the time. I stayed by his side, holding his hand and putting cool cloths on his forehead. As I sat and watched his handsome features twisted in pain, I spent a lot of time thinking about this son, the first child God had given me.

He looked so much like pictures I had seen of Mike as a child: the same tousled gold hair and mischievous blue eyes, the same sun-bronzed complexion dotted with freckles. How badly I had wanted my firstborn to be a son, and how delighted Mike and I had been with our plump baby boy.

But oh, how frightened I had been of him. "What have I gotten myself into?" I used to wonder in desperation. "I don't think I'm cut out to be a mother!" He was so tiny, and he cried all the time. I was certain I was going to hear those demanding screams waking me up every morning for the rest of my life.

As babies always do, Mark grew up entirely too fast. He was headstrong and difficult, and I was so young and so very inexperienced. I tried so hard, but Mark always made me feel like I had failed as a mother. I was nearly always at a loss as to how to handle him in any given situation.

When Mark was four, he was diagnosed as hyperkinetic. We learned that something was just not quite right in his brain; but no one seemed to know why this was so. I had had a normal pregnancy, and Mark had been delivered normally also. Doctors still do not know why some people's brains malfunction as Mark's does (although there are some theories). The one thing the doctor could tell us was that it had nothing to do with intelligence. There was no doubt about it: Mark was a bright boy. Hyperkinetic children usually are; in fact, many outstanding world leaders are thought to have been hyperkinetic as children. We were told that Mark had a bright future, if we could only channel him in the right direction.

I remembered the day Dr. Marshall had given us Mark's diagnosis. It had been quite a shock, but at the same time I had felt as if a huge weight of guilt had been lifted off my shoulders. "It's not my fault! It's not my fault," I had cried over and over again to myself in the car on the way home. "Thank God, it's not my fault!"

At nine years of age, Mark was still often headstrong and difficult, but he was a smart boy and was very affectionate. And, most important of all, he had loved Jesus from the time he had asked him into his heart at the age of five. Mike and I firmly believe that God has a beautiful plan for Mark's life.

"Lord Jesus," I cried silently in that hospital room, "I love this little boy so much! Lord, sometimes I don't think I've been a very good mother to him, but I've tried! I've really tried! I know you wouldn't have given him to me if you hadn't thought I could take good care of him. Lord, I don't know what's the matter with Mark, but you do. Please heal him, Lord. Please!"

"The Lord also will be a stronghold for the oppressed, a stronghold in times of trouble, and those who know Thy name will put their trust in Thee; For Thou, O Lord, hast not forsaken those who seek Thee" (Psalm 9:9, 10).

Mark remained in the hospital for three days, and then spent two weeks at home in bed. It took him another month to get his strength back, but we never found out what had made him so deathly ill. There is, of course, no way to prove my theory; but I firmly believe that Mark had meningitis and that the Lord healed him.

"But certainly God has heard; He has given heed to the voice of my prayer. Blessed be God, who has not turned away my prayer, nor his lovingkindness from me" (Psalm 66:19, 20).

I feel so strongly that God healed Mark in response to the many prayers offered for his life. I am certain he healed our precious Shannon, and I know that he saved Tara's life and restored to her intelligence and the ability to speak.

God is a miracle worker, and I know from personal experience that he is performing miracles in the world today just as he did in Bible times. I know that God heals in answer to prayer, and I know that he has anointed certain individuals with healing ministries. I immediately think of Oral Roberts and the late Kathryn Kuhlman, at whose service the Lord touched Tara's speech. But even so, it is Jesus, through the power of the Holy Spirit, who heals. There is really only one true faith healer: Jesus.

But I also know that God is not limited to using only certain people in a ministry of healing. Because he is all-powerful, God can use any channel he so desires in order to accomplish his plans. One of my favorite people in the whole world, Eleanor Lau, has often been used of God for the healing of the sick. I will never forget this story which she told me several years ago. She had argued with one of her teenaged children and was feeling remorseful. "Lord," she had prayed, "how can you ever use such a broken, imperfect vessel as me?"

"Eleanor," came the answer, "in my business, I can use a sieve!"

If God had to wait for someone perfect to use, he wouldn't ever get anything done. There is no one perfect on this side of heaven! All he really needs is a yielded spirit.

When Mark was seven, he had his tonsils taken out. Mike and I had arrived at the hospital very early that morning so we could be with him before he went into surgery. As we were walking into the pediatric ward, a young father was carrying his four-year-old son out to their car.

The boy had been the victim of a rare disease called epiglottitus, in which the epiglottis swells and closes off the air passage in the throat. If not treated immediately, death by suffocation can result. Various degrees of brain damage can occur if the victim is partially suffocated and then revived. Fortunately, this little boy had received medical care early. The doctors had performed a tracheotomy, making an artificial opening below the epiglottis so the child could breathe. He looked very weak, but was recovered sufficiently to be allowed to go home.

Mark was taken down for surgery, and Mike and I waited in the lobby while he was in the operating and recovery rooms. When we returned once more to the chidren's wing of the hospital, the air was heavy with the sounds of gasping and choking. Hysterical sobs thrust their way through whenever there was enough breath to expel them. Someone was fighting for air, and it sounded like a losing battle!

My eyes darted about the room and soon spotted the small warrior. Over in the corner, encased in an oxygen tent, a little blond baby boy who looked about a year and a half was frantically grasping at the metal bars of his bed. He was wearing only a diaper and his nose was running. Big tears ran down his plump little cheeks and splashed onto his bare chest. It was a heartwrenching sight.

As soon as I got a chance, I asked a nurse what was wrong with him and was amazed to hear that he also had epiglottitis. "He's the brother of the other little boy," she explained. "It's the strangest thing, because epiglottitis isn't contagious. His doctor is planning to perform a tracheotomy this afternoon," she continued. "It's a shame," she shook her head. "He's so little."

My heart was touched by that baby's plight as it has been few times in my life. Even from Mark's room down the hall I could hear his convulsive breathing and frenzied crying. He was so sick and so scared. Mark was asleep nearly all day, so I just sat by his bed and prayed and prayed for that baby.

After I had been praying for an hour or so, the Lord began speaking to me. In fact, you might say we had an argument!

"Donna," he said, "you go tell that baby's mother that you're praying for him."

"But, Lord," I answered, "she'll think I'm crazy. I can't just walk in there and tell her I'm praying for her baby! What will she think? She's probably not a Christian; maybe she doesn't even believe in God. I'd be too embarrassed! You know how shy I am, Lord. How could you even suggest such a crazy scheme?"

"Donna—you'd better do it!"

"No, Lord. I can't."

"Yes, you can!"

And so it went. I must have argued with God for well over an hour. I wasn't about to humble myself and go in there and look like a fool. Not me! I was smarter than that!

Meanwhile, the baby was sounding worse and worse. Finally I couldn't stand it any longer. "OK, Lord, I give up. I'll go in and make an idiot of myself if you want me to. Only please—don't bother me anymore!"

Going into that baby's room was one of the hardest things I've ever had to do. It was completely contrary to my nature, and I wouldn't have done it for anyone but God. I wouldn't even have done it for him if he hadn't completely worn me down and refused to take "no" for an answer. I crept into the child's room as quietly as possible, hoping maybe his mother wouldn't notice me. But she did.

I introduced myself to her and explained that my son was down the hall, having just had his tonsils removed. I told her I had been listening to her baby all day and that I really had a burden on my heart for him. "I've been praying for him for hours," I said. "But I'd really like to pray for him by name. What is his name?"

Her tired face brightened. "Christopher," she said. "Thank you so much for praying. I really appreciate it."

I returned to Mark's room and continued my prayers for Christopher. In a little while, Mark began to come out of the anesthesia and demanded my attention. A couple of hours later, as he was eating a popsicle, I realized that I no longer heard little Christopher's crying and wondered if he had been taken down the hall for surgery.

I looked up and saw the baby's mother standing in the doorway. "Come here," she beckoned to me, smiling broadly. She led me to Christopher's room, and to my astonishment he was sitting up in bed playing with some toys. He was breathing normally and was no longer in the oxygen tent. He turned to me and gave me a big smile.

"It was like a miracle," his mother said. "He started to improve right after you told me you were praying for him. Isn't it wonderful?"

I glanced from face to face. God did it!

That's the only time God has ever used me as a channel for someone's healing. And to think I nearly muffed it up through disobedience! It will always be one of the most outstanding experiences of my life. Few things have ever made me so happy.

To God be the glory!

As the mother of a crippled child, I hear a lot about healing. I get letters from people all over the country telling me about this faith healer and that faith healer. One woman wanted us to drive Tara all the way to Denver, Colorado, to attend a miracle service being conducted by a man she listened to on the radio. "God is really with him," she urged. "You must take Tara there." Equally well-meaning souls have asked us to take Tara other places, both near and far, to see their own favorite healer. Each one can't understand why we don't rush right over with Tara immediately.

It's so hard to explain, and I guess I don't completely understand it myself. We have taken Tara to miracle services, not once but several times. She has been to famous ones like Kathryn Kuhlman at the Shrine and Ralph Wilkerson at Melodyland. She has been to see others whose names I can't even recall. She's been anointed with oil and prayed for by the church elders twice. I have read countless books on the subject and have tried at one time or another each of the different methods advised to insure healing.

These formulas, which often contradict each other, are all said to bring about the desired results. And I think perhaps this is the problem. You can't "bring about" a result with God. If God wants something to happen, he brings it about. He doesn't have to rely on people following a certain formula in order to work a miracle. If he wants to work a miracle, *he* works it! He's not even limited by whether or not there is faith present.

Mike and I have faith that God performs miracles today. We've seen miracles and have even been a part of some. Tara herself has complete trust in God and a perfect faith that God performs miracles of healing. I believe God heals, because the Bible says so. And even if I had never seen a miracle healing, I would still have complete faith in the miracle-working power of God.

The fact is, God does not heal everyone who asks him to. In the miracle services I have attended, even though many go forward to attest to healing, they are only a small number compared to those who are not healed. As far as I have been able to tell from my own experiences and studies (and I have heard some of the great men and women who have been instruments of God's healing power say the same), God seems to be no respecter of persons when he heals. This should come as no surprise, really, because it fits in with the fact that God loves all people equally.

"I have seen everything during my lifetime of futility; there is a righteous man who perishes in his righteousness, and there is a wicked man who prolongs his life in his wickedness" (Ecclesiastes 7:15).

"For He causes His sun to rise on the evil and the good, and sends rain on the righteous and the unrighteous" (Matthew 5:45).

In *Daughter of Destiny,* Jamie Buckingham's biography of Kathryn Kuhlman, he speaks of asking Miss Kuhlman why some people were not healed during her services. He quotes her as saying, " 'The only honest answer I can give is: I do not know. Only God knows, and who can fathom the mind of God? When I was twenty years old, I could have given you all the answers. My theology was straight and I was sure that if you followed certain rules, worked hard enough, obeyed all the commandments, and had yourself in a certain spiritual state, God would heal you. But God never responds to man's demands to prove Himself.' "

I don't know why God heals some and not others. How can I, a mere mortal, ever hope to plumb the mind of God? God knows the end from the beginning; I don't. He can see around the corner and down the street, while my vision is limited to my own front yard. All I know is, God has a plan for everyone; and it is his business, not mine, who he heals.

I believe God has the power to heal Tara. I believe he loves Tara more than I ever could. I believe he wants only the very best for my daughter. I also believe that God knows better than I do what the very best is for Tara. I say that the very best for Tara would have been that she never have been injured in the first place. From a human standpoint, I think we would all agree.

But it was through Tara's accident and subsequent handicaps that Tara herself and our entire family have come to know Jesus in a personal way. I wouldn't trade knowing Jesus for a whole house full of normal little girls! And I know that Tara wouldn't trade her relationship with Christ for arms and legs that work. Had Tara never been hurt, I would never have written the book *Tara* which has been instrumental in changing the lives of so many people. In some cases *Tara* was a seed planted, at other times it worked like sunshine and water to cause a seed to grow, and in still others, it actually was used to reap the harvest. I don't know if it was God's perfect will that planned Tara's accident or whether it was only in his permissive will. He certainly knew about it beforehand, because he warned Mike about it in a dream. At any rate, God, as only he can, was able to take a tragedy and turn it into a blessing for others.

Will God heal Tara? Only God knows. Only

God knows the plan he has for Tara's life. The Bible says in Jeremiah 29:11:

"For I know the plans that I have for you," declares the Lord, "plans for welfare and not for calamity to give you a future and a hope."

I believe God has a wonderful plan for Tara's life. I personally hope that his plan includes her complete healing, whether that healing comes gradually through therapy and surgery or whether it is instantaneous.

One day Terry was talking to Tara about the healing she so desires. "Tara," he said, "God can do anything, and if he wanted to, he could make you walk right now. But, for reasons only he knows, he may wish to wait. In fact, God may be performing his miracle right now, but slowly. Suppose," he continued, "that we were sitting outside and saw a little green leaf poke its head out of the ground. Then right in front of our eyes it began to grow and grow, until in a matter of seconds it had grown into a full-size tree. We would say it was a miracle. But you know, each tree that exists today did the same thing; not in seconds, but in years. So actually each tree is a miracle; the only difference is in the time it took each to grow. God could make you walk right now; or he could heal you gradually, like the tree grows. Either way, it will be a miracle, won't it?"

But perhaps God's plan does not include healing. What then? The reason for Tara's existence, as it is for every person, is to glorify God and enjoy him forever. Perhaps God, in his wisdom, knows that Tara can reflect his character and nature better from a wheelchair than she can standing on her own two feet. Maybe he feels that she can know and love him better confined to a wheelchair than if she were up running around.

Jesus is called the Good Shepherd. In Bible times, when a shepherd had a little lamb that was particularly rambunctious and forever wandering off and getting lost, the shepherd would break the lamb's leg so that it was unable to walk. Then he would tenderly carry the little lamb on his own shoulders and lovingly nurse it back to health. In this way, the lamb grew to love the shepherd so much that he never wanted to stray from him again. I believe that Tara is one of the Good Shepherd's special little lambs. I know she will be perfect eventually, even if she has to wait until she gets to heaven.

CHAPTER SEVEN
Christmas Trip

In early December—after Mark's illness—it was time for Tara to return to the Institutes in Philadelphia once more. She was going about four times a year for five-day visits in which she was reevaluated and given a new therapy program. She had been on a plateau for several months, and Mike and I both felt she would receive a poor report.

Mike has always been so good to take Tara to Philadelphia for me. He knows that the week Tara is gone gives me a wonderful respite from the constant task of caring for her. Not only that, but it gives me a perfect opportunity to spend extra time with the other children. I mapped out for myself a week of special activities, including Christmas shopping and baking cookies.

By this time, we had begun to receive letters

from people who had read our book *Tara*. It was so thrilling to hear from people all over the country who had been touched by the courage of our special little girl. One of the letters had come from a family in Pennsylvania. Claire Lunde is a nurse, and her husband, Al, teaches music at Philadelphia College of the Bible. With their daughters, they live in Ardmore, a suburb of Philadelphia. They had read our book and had fallen in love with Tara. Would we like to stay with them during Tara's next visit to the Institutes? Would we! Mike and Tara were warmly taken into their home. The Lundes raise Himalayan cats, and Tara loved playing with the kittens.

Tara's report, as we had anticipated, was not good. Despite the hours and hours of therapy she was receiving daily, her body remained stiff and she was still unable to do more than crawl on her tummy at a snail's pace across the floor. She was so sweet and tried so hard! What else could we do for her?

Glenn Doman, the Institutes' director, was working on a new project. He is forever trying to find new ways of helping the brain-injured children he loves so much. Children with brain injuries are notoriously poor breathers. Their lungs are weak and undeveloped; and their respiration, like everything else about them, is uncoordinated and inconsistent. What would happen if he could pattern correct breathing into the children?

Like the scientist he is, he set about trying to find out. He established a respiratory patterning department on an experimental basis in order to investigate his theory. He suggested we bring Tara back for a week in which she could be exposed to regular periods of respiratory patterning.

Mike and I were anxious to give it a try and decided to send Tara back before Christmas. Since he couldn't spare any more time away from his work, it was decided that I should take Tara this time. It was to be an interesting trip, because I was to have my first flight in a corporate jet.

Mike knows Jay Reed of Fluor Corporation. They have their own jet airplane which regularly flies employees around the country. He had previously told us that anytime it was flying to the East Coast and had two empty seats, we were welcome to fly with them. Their flight schedule had never coincided with one of Tara's appointments before, but this time it did.

It was a beautiful plane, seating around twelve people. The interior was richly paneled and decorated, and Tara and I settled down on a chocolate-brown suede couch. It was just beginning to mist slightly in Los Angeles, and we knew that a full-fledged storm was on its way. Tara and I were the only passengers; the plane was flying to San Francisco to pick up some businessmen before heading for Pennsylvania.

In California, a winter rainstorm usually comes out of the north and is often accompanied by high winds. Such was the case with this one, and we flew right into it. I hate to admit it, but I really don't like airplanes very much at all. I am usually sure that once I get up in one, I will never set foot on the ground again.

As a Christian, I find it extremely embarrassing that I should have such an excessive fear. "Perfect love casts out fear" (1 John 4:18) is one of my favorite verses of Scripture. I'm never quite sure whose perfect love it talks about. I know my own love isn't perfect and never could be, so I figure it must mean God's love which is always perfect. So when I'm up in a plane, I always tell myself that God has perfect love for me; and if I will let him, he will cast out all my fears. Then I just empty my mind of everything else and concentrate on God's great love for me.

During this particular hour's flight, however, I was so terrified that I was unable to concentrate on God's love. Gale winds whipped the small plane into wild plunges and loops, and we pitched to and fro as machine and nature met each other in riotous conflict. A volley of raindrops the size of Ping-Pong balls assaulted us from all sides, buffeting us with such intensity that I thought for sure we would be crushed from the sheer force of all that water. I was sure my time had come; I knew I would never see my husband and other children again!

Tara had a bad cold, and she was crying because her ears hurt. I swore if we ever made it to San Francisco, I was getting off that plane and pushing Tara down Coast Highway in her wheelchair all the way to Los Angeles! I didn't know it at the time, but two private planes, battered by the heavy winds, collided in the air over Santa Barbara that day. My fears had been well-founded.

It was pouring down rain when we landed in San Francisco, and I sat trembling on the elegant suede couch. What should I do? I didn't want to fly anymore! But I knew I didn't really have a choice; Tara must be taken to Philadelphia. I'd just have to try to be brave. "Lord, on my own I am nothing. Please see me through!"

The plane filled with businessmen, and we took off toward the East. We had one of the smoothest flights I've ever been on. What a contrast; what a blessing!

Tara and I spent a few days in New Jersey with our friends, Lee and Dave Bulfin. It was such a pleasure to relax in the quiet of their calm home. There are many adjectives to describe our home, but calm isn't one of them! Tara and I were reading *Little House on the Prairie,* and I sewed five green velvet Christmas stockings.

We rode into Philadelphia by Amtrak and were met at the train station by Claire Lunde and her two daughters. I am so inept at handling traveling details. I always forget to tip the porters and usually get lost trying to find my way out of the terminal. With Tara and her wheelchair, it is even more difficult. God has been so good to me and has provided someone to meet me and look after me every single time I've taken Tara to Philadelphia.

Claire drove us through the iron gates of the Institutes and up to the beautiful old mansion that was to be our home for the next week.

Tara was delighted to be back so soon, and to me it was like coming back to the home of an old friend. I love everyone, from Helen and Doris who sit at the front door in their wheelchairs and greet people and work the switchboard, right up to Glenn Doman, the director.

It was a little scary, being there by myself with Tara for a whole week, but I needn't have worried. We soon made friends with the other parents and children. There was Lorenzo from Italy and his pretty mom, Daniella, and her friend Rosa. They had been at the Institutes since August, working daily with Lorenzo. Jeffery and his mother from New York were there. Jeff had serious breathing difficulties, and the respiratory patterning at the Institutes was helping to save his life. Schinizi and his family were there all the way from Japan. His father, a medical doctor, was studying the Institutes' methods with the hope of establishing an Institute in Japan. Little Schinizi, with his big black eyes, had progressed so well on the patterning program. How wonderful if other brain-injured Japanese children could receive treatment in their own country. Jerry, a young man from Ireland who helped the Institutes on a volunteer basis, had brought a large group of new patients from the Emerald Isle and was overseeing their needs. In all, we were a very international group, bound together by the common tie of brain injury.

Tara and I reported to the respiratory patterning department on the second floor of the old mansion right after breakfast on

Monday morning. Mike had tried to explain to me what the respirators looked like, but it had been difficult for me to picture them in my mind. They were located in a large room with doors that opened out onto a beautiful balcony. The room was full of pattern tables, which look rather like examining tables in a doctor's office. On each table was a yellow metal mesh cage and quite a bit of clear, heavy plastic. There was a little stand behind each table, housing the actual respirator unit which looked rather like a canister vacuum cleaner.

Dr. Peters, with her businesslike German accent, assigned Tara a table toward the back of the room overlooking the balcony. She took Tara's pulse, checked her heartbeat with a stethoscope, noted her respiration rate, and wrote all the information down on her chart.

Then we laid Tara down on her back and put the wire cage over her torso from her neck to her hips. The heavy plastic bag was then brought up over the cage and clipped together so that everything but Tara's head was encased in airtight plastic. Then Dr. Peters turned on the respirator itself and adjusted its pressure. It immediately began its rhythmic pulsing, drawing air from the bag and then releasing the suction. When the air is drawn out of the plastic bag, it creates a vacuum within the bag. Since at this point the air pressure surrounding Tara's chest is less than the air pressure in the room, air is automatically forced into Tara's lungs. This process is repeated over and over, patterning correct breathing.

I thought maybe Tara would look or act

differently in the respirator. I expected her to have difficulty talking because of the pressure. But she acted and spoke as if lying flat on her back in a respirator were the most normal thing in the world. It is really a blessing that Tara is so adaptable and adjusts so easily to new situations.

"Hi, Lorenzo," she beamed at the frail little boy lying on the table across the aisle from her. He turned toward Tara and flashed her a big grin. "How are you today?" she asked, then answered herself, "Fine, I bet." The fact that Lorenzo couldn't speak didn't bother Tara one bit. After all, he understood her. She knew that, and that was all that mattered. She could keep up enough conversation for the both of them.

The room was very warm and the rhythmic swish-swish of the respirator was very lulling to me. I had a terrible time trying to stay awake. Every time Tara was in the respirator, I had to fight to keep my eyes open. But not Tara! If she wasn't engaged in animated conversation with Lorenzo, she wanted to be read to. We read all the way through *Little House on the Prairie* that week, as well as numerous shorter children's books I had brought. My throat ached from all that talking!

Tara started out by spending forty-five minutes at a time in the respirator, and this was increased by small increments until she was able to stay in it for three hours all at once by the end of the week.

At the end of each period, Dr. Peters examined Tara again and noted her findings on Tara's chart. When the week was over, they would graph the results and get an overall picture of what, if any, changes were occurring.

In between periods of respiration, Tara and I, as well as the other children, went across the grounds to the Mobility Building. It was bitter cold outside, and Tara and I really had to bundle up before dashing over the frozen grass.

Art Sandler, mobility director, was there busily running from one child to another, encouraging, prodding, cajoling, loving, making suggestions, and pushing each child to his maximum. Each of the children needed four five-minute crawling patterns a day; and we mothers made up the patterning teams. Tara was the largest of the children and the only one who needed four people to pattern her; the others only needed patterning teams of three. We put the children on their tummies on the patterning tables and took turns patterning them, one woman at the child's head and one at each side to move his arms and legs. Tara's left side, because it was so stiff, required two people to move it, one person for the arm and one for the leg.

Since it was so close to Christmas, we usually sang Christmas carols to help keep the rhythm and to pass the time. Over and over we sang the old familiar tunes, each one of us singing in her own language. What a joy it was to hear songs like "Oh Come, All Ye Faithful" and "Silent Night" sung in English, Italian, and Japanese simultaneously. It reminded me of the opening line of the popular song "I'd Like to Teach the World to Sing in Perfect Harmony," and I thought of how people all over the world are united in the love they have for their children. I thought about that concept a little more and was made freshly aware that we are all God's children, and that he desires to unite us all in the love of his precious Son, born into the world on that first Christmas so long ago.

Jeff's mother brought construction paper and began to cut out Christmas decorations to put on the walls and windows of the Mobility Building and the respiratory patterning room. She fashioned little bells and stars and Santa Clauses, which brought such cheer and Christmas spirit to us there.

One day just as we were getting the children settled in their respirators after lunch, Daniella began jumping up and down in excitement and shouting "Nieve! Nieve!" I looked out the window and saw snow drifting silently through the frosty sky. "Tara! Tara! It's snowing! Look!" I exclaimed as I turned her head so she too could see God working his winter fantasies. It never snows in Mission Viejo, California, and that was the closest thing to a white Christmas that Tara and I had ever seen.

"Oh, I want to go outside!" Tara shrieked with glee as she kicked her legs in delight. But Dr. Peters looked firm. Tara was in her respirator, and she was going to stay there until her time was up whether she liked it or not. Rosa, Daniella, and I went out onto the balcony and caught snow in our open mouths and cupped hands. I made a snowball and carried it in to Tara, who was thrilled and wanted to taste it and touch it. But it was only a brief flurry; and by the time Tara was out of her respirator, it had stopped snowing and what had been on the ground had melted.

The snow incident was much like Tara's entire life has been since her accident. She must sit on the sidelines and watch, but can never really play the game. And yet she is amazingly content and patient as she watches the world go by. I think her cheerful attitude is one of God's special blessings to our family. And what a lesson we can all learn from her!

It is good to have goals and to strive to achieve them. But it is also good to be patient and happy with whatever situation God puts us in for the moment. It is important to concentrate on what we have rather than what we have not. For we really only live in the now; we need to learn to be content with the way we are now and enjoy each moment to the fullest as it is occurring. As the plaque in my entrance hall says, "Bloom Where You Are Planted." Glorify God in whatever situation he has placed you. "In everything give thanks; for this is God's will for you in Christ Jesus" (1 Thessalonians 5:18).

This is one of the main reasons why I am a basically happy person in spite of my circumstances. My happiness doesn't have to depend on my circumstances; it rests on God. I don't have to be feeling guilty about something I did yesterday, because I know God has forgiven me. And I don't have to worry about what is going to happen to me tomorrow, because I know God will work out all things for my good. That only leaves me with today. Do I have problems? Do I get worried? You bet! Do I always rise above my problems? Not always. But I think the key is that I always keep my problems in perspective. And I think Tara does too.

Wednesday morning Mike called me with some startling news. "Mark is in the hospital," he reported.

"Oh, no! Not again!" I gasped. "What is it?" I could hardly stand to think of my little boy all alone in the hospital while I was 3,000 miles away.

It seems that Mark had been downstairs in the kitchen frying bacon for breakfast while Mike was upstairs shaving. When the bacon was done, Mark decided to pour the boiling grease into a jar, not realizing he should wait until it had cooled. The skillet handle was greasy and slipped out of Mark's hands, throwing hot oil all over his right arm and side.

Mike had raced him to the nearby hospital where doctors put him directly into ice water treatments. The burns were third degree, he said, and Mark would have to stay all day and night in the hospital.

I felt outraged that Mike could have let Mark hurt himself so badly. "How could you!" I demanded, "Weren't you watching him?" And immediately I felt ashamed that I'd lashed out at my husband so cruelly. I realized how badly he was feeling about Mark hurting himself while under his care. Mike needed my support, not my condemnation! And yet how often we are so anxious to blame someone for accidents. How much better it is for us to support each other and attack the problem rather than to ignore the problem and attack each other. "I'm sorry, Michael. Please forgive me."

I was so far away. Physically there was nothing I could do for Mark. Thank goodness for prayer! I could take Mark and his burns to God. God could see to Mark's needs even if I couldn't! So I prayed that Mark might not be in too much pain, and that he might not feel scared and alone since Mike was unable to stay with him in the hospital. As it turned out, Terry went over and spent the day with Mark; and, amazingly, the pain was not more than he was able to bear.

His burns bled and oozed for months. I thought they would never heal, and when they finally did, they left horrible scars. Someday Mark will probably require skin grafts to repair them.

The week we spent at the Institutes was invigorating to both Tara and me. We made so many new friends and had such good times. One night we went to see the movie *Dumbo,* with Schinizi and Lorenzo and some of the neurologically handicapped college students who attend classes at the Institutes. It was such a touching movie that Tara was moved to tears. Little Schinizi, who at three-and-a-half was just learning to say a few words but could understand English, Japanese, and some Italian, really opened up and cried during the sad parts. Tara looked over at him through her tears and said, "Don't cry Schinizi. It's OK."

One day, as Tara was on the floor watching Lorenzo being patterned, she complained that she was unable to see him well while lying on her tummy. "Let me get on my hands and knees," she begged. Tara was able to get into a sort of semi-quad position. If I tucked her legs up under her bottom and placed her hands in front of her, she could, with some effort, push up a little on her hands and get her head and trunk up off the floor. I positioned her in this manner and she pushed right up. Then she astounded me by pushing up until her arms were straight, eventually taking her hands off the floor and straightening her back until she was actually sitting up on her knees! It took her several minutes to perform this task, and it was very difficult for her. She was only able to maintain it for a few seconds before she fell back down on her hands again. The amazing thing was that she didn't lose her balance, so she was able to raise her hands and sit again several times.

She was so excited, she couldn't stop laughing. I was so excited, I couldn't stop crying! To actually see my little girl sit up, all by herself, no matter how briefly, was an event I had dreamed of night and day for four and a half years! I had almost given up the hope that it would ever happen, and yet here it was. A miracle!

Our last night in Philadelphia was spent downtown looking at all the beautiful Christmas decorations. The air was so cold and frosty, and the stores were all decorated with garlands of fresh pine boughs. It really felt and smelled like Christmas, and Tara and I loved it. The Lunde family walked us all over and showed us the best of this historic city by starlight. Tara had a wonderful time, and was so animated and full of conversation that she attracted the attention of a rather intoxicated hobo. He was fascinated by her, and she was too young to know the dangers of a big city after dark. She smiled and flirted with him, and he followed us for fifteen or twenty minutes before wandering off into the darkness.

When we returned to their home, the Lundes said they had a Christmas gift for the children. They brought out a large box wrapped in red Christmas paper and ribbon. I helped Tara open it, and what should peek its head out from under the lid but a beautiful little kitten! Tara screamed in delight as we sat the little ball of fur on her lap. "Oh, I love him! I love him! Thank you!" she bubbled as she buried her head in his long soft fur. His name, we learned, was Peanut.

The next morning, early, we packed Peanut in a traveling box at the airport and took him on the plane with us. The stewardesses all fell in love with him, and sometimes I took him out of his box and let Tara hold him on her lap. It was such a smooth flight and the stewardesses had been so nice that when the plane touched ground in Los Angeles, everyone on board broke into a round of applause.

Mike and Mark met us at the airport. We had been gone ten days, and there was so much to catch up on. Of special import to me was Mark's arm, which looked like a piece of raw meat under the bandages.

And I could hardly wait to see Christa! Ten days was such a long time to be away from a twenty-month-old. I was so anxious to gather her up in my arms. We drove straight to the

Bjorklunds' home where she was staying, and she came bounding out the front door when she heard our knock. Her blue eyes sparkling and her dimples flashing, she tossed her blonde curls as I gathered her up in my arms. "Mommy, Mommy!" she cried in delight. And then she spotted Tara. "Tara! Sister!" and she wriggled onto Tara's lap. "Christa!" Tara was laughing and crying. How those two little girls love each other!

I thought back to the time when I first learned I was expecting Christa. I had been totally horrified at the thought of a baby and was certain it would disrupt our lives completely. And yet how well God knew what our family needed.

We were not even aware of the void, but God knew how desperately we needed a perfectly normal little girl. I cannot even begin to put into words all that Christa means to me. She is like my proof that there is normalcy in the world, and that it is not completely out of my grasp. When I watch her running and playing and doing all the things all the other little girls do, it makes me so grateful to God for giving her to me. How thankful I am to have a child that I don't have to really worry about on a deep level.

The love that Christa and Tara share is a beautiful thing to behold, surely a gift from God. They have been especially devoted to each other since Christa's infancy. Christa has literally grown up in Tara's therapy workroom. It was there, surrounded by patterners, that she learned to crawl and creep, to take her first step. She crawled with Tara when Tara crawled, and clapped her chubby little hands for her when she did an especially good job. When I would take the two girls out together, I was unable to push toddling Christa in a stroller, because I needed both hands to push Tara's wheelchair.

When she first learned to walk, Christa began the habit of walking next to Tara and holding either her sister's hand or the arm of her wheelchair. Over the years, she has become Tara's closest friend and best playmate. She is like a bridge between Tara's world of brain injury and the normal world of children outside. Through Christa, Tara can sometimes make it all the way across the bridge to the sunlight on the other side.

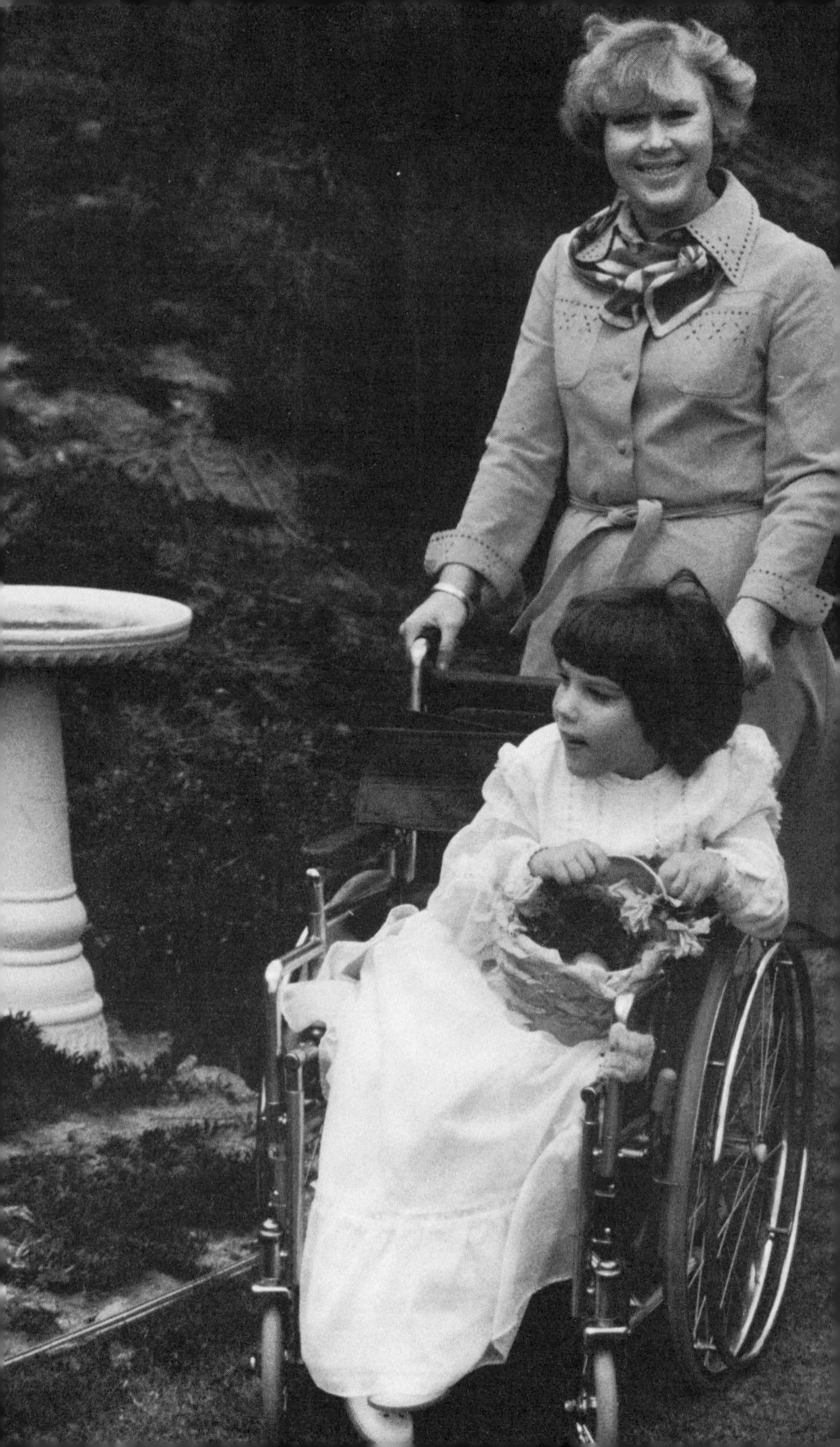

CHAPTER EIGHT
Of People and Places

Once home, we plunged into last-minute Christmas preparations with fervor. My parents, Claire and Doug Henson, were flying out from Texas to spend a few days with us; and Mike's folks, Marge and Bud, would be down from Northern California. The children were all so thrilled to be seeing both sets of grandparents.

One of my greatest regrets is that our parents live so far away that the children rarely see them. I think grandparents are so special and play such an important part in children's lives. I have so many cherished memories of my own grandparents, it hurts me to think that my children will have so few.

That is why I am especially pleased that God has supplied substitute grandparents for my children in the form of Terry's parents, Vivian and Sam Patané. They have helped baby-sit, had the children over to spend the night, and given them special grandparent-type treats on birthdays and holidays.

One day shortly before Christmas, the postman delivered two large boxes addressed to Tara. I carried them up to her workroom, and she began squealing with delight. "Whitey! Packages from Whitey!"

The previous summer, Mike had taken Tara to Philadelphia for evaluation and then gone on to New York City to transact some business for Hour of Power. On Sunday morning, he and Tara had been sitting in the coffee shop of the Americana Hotel having breakfast. A casually dressed, gray-haired man was sitting alone at a table nearby. He noticed Tara and smiled at her warmly.

For Tara, this was an open invitation to flirt. She began to smile broadly and to talk with the man in the delightful way that only little girls can. He responded and when he had eaten his meal, he came over and asked about Tara. "My name is Whitey Gullons. What room are you staying in?" he asked. "I'd like to send Tara a gift."

Mike was taken by surprise and wasn't quite sure what to say. Nevertheless, he told the man their room number, thinking that he would probably never hear from Mr. Gullons again.

Later in the day, however, the bellman brought a wrapped package to the door, and Tara was delighted to find a little glass animal and a glass globe filled with red roses from Whitey.

Whitey saw Tara only that one brief time, yet he has never forgotten her. Not a holiday goes by but that he sends her gifts for the occasion. Thanksgiving, Christmas, Valentine's Day, Easter, Tara's birthday; each time boxes of treats arrive. Sometimes he will send a gift just to show he is thinking of her. He always puts so much thought into the things he sends, so that each package is full of special items just guaranteed to charm a little girl.

What would make a man be so thoughtful and caring of a child he has only met once? I can only think that God touched him in a special way to give him such love for Tara. Whitey and his gifts have brightened up many a lonely hour for her, and we are so grateful to him and to our Heavenly Father from whom generosity comes.

Christmas Eve found us at Garden Grove Community Church's beautiful candlelight service. The sanctuary was lit with hundreds of candles and fresh pine garlands everywhere. The trumpets sounded, the bells rang, and thousands of voices lifted up their songs of praise to Christ the King. I marveled at God's great love in sending us Jesus. To think that Jesus left the glory that was his in heaven and humbled himself to be born into the world as a human infant! As a mother, I realize how completely helpless babies are, and it never ceases to amaze me that the Creator of the universe would allow himself to become totally dependent upon his own creatures.

It has become our custom to gather the children together in our bedroom on Christmas morning for devotions before going downstairs to open gifts. We read a portion of the Christmas story from Luke, pray, and then all sing Happy Birthday to Jesus. In today's Santa Claus-saturated society, Mike and I feel it is so important to stress to our children the real reason why we celebrate Christmas. In all the hustle-bustle, it is sometimes entirely too easy to forget. Eleanor Lau always says, "God gave us Christmas, but Satan invented the Christmas rush!"

After Christmas, we settled back into our normal routine once more. Mike and I arose at 7 A.M., showered and dressed, and woke up Mark and Tara. Tara, of course, had to be bathed, dressed, taken to her potty, and fed her breakfast. Then I would brush her long dark hair and put it into braids. Mike would leave to drive Mark to school on his way to work.

By this time it would be 9:00, time for the first patterners to arrive. They would put Tara through her paces while I got Christa up, bathed, dressed, and fed her. Carol Mogan, Tara's wonderful home teacher, came at 10:00 to spend an hour working with her in scholastic areas. I took this opportunity to clean the kitchen, make beds, and fold laundry. At 11:00 Christa and I went into Tara's workroom. Christa played, and I gave Tara therapy from 11:00 until 12:00. At noon we broke for lunch. I had an hour in which to prepare three different meals (why is it that we never all want to eat the same things?), feed myself, feed Tara, and clean up Christa. Christa could feed herself;

but, oh how that little face got smeared with peanut butter!

At 1:00, more women arrived to help me give Tara her afternoon programing. I worked with Tara until 2:00, at which time I put Christa down for a nap and went downstairs to greet Mark when he came home from school. I tried to have some time to spend with him each afternoon when he first came home, to talk about his day and to fix him a snack. After Mark had eaten, he was usually anxious to go outside and play with his friends for the rest of the afternoon. How I wish I had his energy!

I was usually back upstairs by 2:45 and worked with Tara until 5:30. Christa, who woke up around 4:00, played in the workroom with some of the children who often came with their mothers. It was not at all unusual for us to have as many as fifteen people at a time in Tara's workroom, including patterners and their children of all ages.

We carried Tara downstairs at the end of her workday and let her have some free time while I cooked dinner. Sometimes she wanted to draw or play dolls with her sister, and often she liked to watch television. By the time dinner had been eaten and the kitchen cleaned up, it was time to put the children to bed. First Christa, then Tara, and lastly Mark. My mother always used to make bedtime special for me by being especially loving at this time, lingering over prayers and good-night kisses. Mike and I try to do the same; and since I like to sing, I often add a song to our nightly ritual. One of the children's favorites is "Kum Ba Ya," which I always end by singing "Someone's sleeping, Lord, Kum Ba Ya." This is a beautiful song from Africa, and Kum Ba Ya means "come by here."

By the time we had tucked the children into bed, Mike and I were usually exhausted. However, we generally had laundry waiting to be folded, phone calls to be made, or letters to be written. When we finally made it to bed, and I had read my Bible for awhile, sleep came very quickly.

Of course, this was the normal routine. Things could get extremely complicated when someone got sick, or when we had appointments during the day, or when we had company. Mike and I often had to attend evening social gatherings in conjunction with his job at the church, and these also could cause things to get a little hectic.

Worst of all, though, was when Mike had to go out of town on business. Part of his job is to buy air time for the Hour of Power. That means he negotiates contracts with television stations all across the country, and it necessitates quite a bit of traveling.

Managing everything by myself in the evenings sometimes used to be a nightmare for me. It seemed that Tara would always have a terrible accident in her pants at the same time that Christa would fall and hurt herself, and Mark would busy himself seeing how loudly he could get both of them to scream. Predictably the phone or the doorbell would ring right in the middle of all this activity! I would sometimes still be in the kitchen at 11:00, washing dishes.

As Tara began getting heavier, it was harder for me to carry her back and forth in the evenings, too. I thank the Lord for Terry, who often came over and helped me feed the children and put them to bed and clean the kitchen.

I was so thankful that I had finally gotten over my fear of staying alone in the house at night. When Mike first started traveling, I used to lie in my bed in stark terror for hours, listening to the night with the certain knowledge that I would be robbed and mutilated before morning.

I used to keep Mark's baseball bat under the covers on Mike's side of the bed, and my heaviest kitchen skillet under his pillow. Then I got to worrying that if the burglar saw them he might decide to bludgeon me to death with them before I could use them on him. After I became a Christian and heard that the Word of God is sharper than a two-edged sword, I began putting my Bible on Mike's pillow for protection.

It took me a period of four to five years, but I finally overcame this great fear. I realized that even when Mike is home he would be unable to protect the family if someone really wanted to do us harm. I began to see that it is really God who protects us, and I'm sure he watches over us extra carefully when Mike is gone. When I could finally accept this concept, not just intellectually, but emotionally as well, my fear was gone.

One incident that really made me acutely

aware of this fact happened while I was writing the book *Tara*. Mike and I had gone up to the mountains, which are about a two hours' drive from our home, in the month of October. Forest Home Christian Conference Center, where we have spent so many happy weeks vacationing with the children in the summer, had said we could spend a few days in solitude there to get some writing done.

We had always been there for family camp, and the canyon had always been full of people and activity. But at this time, in the middle of an autumn week, the entire camp was deserted. We didn't see another living soul the whole time we were there. This was perfect for our purposes, because we were looking for peace and quiet in which to write.

We had a beautiful cabin overlooking the lake and enjoyed days of sitting outdoors under an umbrella, writing and drinking in the beauty of crisp autumn air and golden trees whispering in the breeze. Our first night there, we fried mountain trout and potatoes for dinner and dutifully put our trash outside in the large barrel provided for that purpose. We relaxed by the fireplace and wrote for a while after dinner, then retired fairly early.

In the middle of the night, I was awakened by the sounds of someone trying to open our bedroom window. Whoever it was was rattling it something fierce. I shot up in bed, absolutely terrified. "Michael! Wake up!" I practically shouted. "Prowlers!" Mike was awake in a flash and immediately grasped the seriousness of the situation.

There we were, miles from nowhere, completely isolated in the pitch-black of a mountain night, with no telephone. And what kind of a person would be breaking into a mountain cabin? Certainly not someone looking for money or jewels. It must be a madman, we both decided.

We tried to remain calm and reassure each other, but we were both scared to death. The "madman" was going from the kitchen door to the front door, frantically turning the knobs. He went from there to the windows again. I don't think there has ever been a time when I have felt in more mortal danger.

We went to the closet to put on our bathrobes, and I put on my tennis shoes in case I had to run for it. Mike got two coathangers for weapons. And we prayed; oh how we prayed! The dreadful break-in attempts continued as we huddled in the hallway.

Finally Mike gathered his courage and went into the kitchen and turned on an outside light in hopes of getting a look at the prowler and maybe scaring him away. Suddenly I heard him begin to laugh uncontrollably.

"Come here!" he called to me. I walked fearfully into the kitchen and peered out the window. I caught my breath and then let out a long sigh of relief. "Raccoons!" we both shouted at once.

Our fears were dispelled immediately, but it took hours for us to calm down. I thought we would never fall back to sleep! The next morning we were both feeling rather sheepish, but our fright had been real. If it had been a real prowler, I don't think we would have reacted any differently.

I've come to the conclusion that what really counts is trusting God and believing that he knows what is best for us. That includes trusting him to give us the grace to live through any trial that may come our way—even raccoons!

Casting all your anxiety upon Him, because He cares for you (1 Peter 5:7).

In late February, the routine was broken once more as both Mike and I took Tara back to Philadelphia for reevaluation. Tara and I had both come down with terrible colds and spent our entire plane ride wiping drippy noses.

Monday was Tara's first day at the Institutes, and Mike suggested I stay in the hotel and rest while he took Tara in for her appointments. I thought it was a wonderful idea and read and napped the entire day. I was so glad I had stayed behind because I was there to receive a very important phone call.

Dr. Schuller keeps a very busy speaking calendar, and the week before he had been in a suburb of Philadelphia speaking for the twenty-fifth anniversary of the Oreland Presbyterian Church. While there he had mentioned to its pastor, Charles Murray, that Mike Nason, his producer, would be in Philadelphia with his daughter and wife the following week.

I was surprised when the phone rang around noon that day, because to my knowledge no one in Philadelphia knew where I was.

"Mrs. Nason!" the friendly voice boomed

when I answered. "Chuck Murray here! My wife and I would like to have you and Mike join us for dinner tonight at our home!"

"Lord," I whispered, "you do plan the most delightful surprises for us when we are least expecting them, don't you?"

Pastor Murray picked me up that evening and drove me to his lovely manse. It was right next to a storybook New England church with a tall white steeple. It was so beautiful and quaint, yet stately, that I fell in love with it at once. It didn't take me much longer than that to love this dynamic preacher and his bubbly blonde wife, Nancy. They were so charming and gracious, and they put me right at ease.

Mike and Tara were kept late at the Institutes waiting for appointments, but they finally arrived in our rented car. Nancy had prepared a delicious roast beef dinner with popovers and all the trimmings. And the conversation was even better than the dinner.

They were, as is everyone, so impressed by Tara's attitude and spirit, and asked many questions. Chuck shared his dreams of growth for his church with Mike, and the evening ended with an invitation for me to attend a women's luncheon on Wednesday.

Early the next morning Mike, Tara, and I were to appear on a Philadelphia television program about our book *Tara*. We were especially excited, because Glenn Doman was also to be a guest. Tara wasn't feeling well, and she sat on the couch next to Mike, her head drooping listlessly. We tried so hard to get her to talk and smile, but she just wouldn't cooperate.

The program broke for a commercial, and Glenn joined us on stage. He leaned over to Tara and whispered something in her ear. She immediately perked up, and began smiling and talking. Mike and I were amazed at the transformation. When the taping was over, we could hardly wait to ask Glenn what he had told Tara to cheer her up so dramatically. He grinned and winked at us, a mischievous twinkle in his blue eyes. "I told her if she didn't smile I was going to break her little neck!"

Tara spent the rest of Tuesday and all day Wednesday working in the Mobility Building at the Institutes. The mobility director, Art, ran from one child to another giving directions, but it was up to Mike and me to actually help Tara perform her tasks. They were hard days, but without the interruptions of children and ringing phones that we had at home.

I was glad to leave Wednesday at noon when Pastor Murray picked me up to take me to the luncheon. Eight of the faithful church workers were there, as well as the church's missionary to Afghanistan. We spent such a pleasant afternoon, and I was once again struck by the fact that Christians everywhere all speak the same language. We are all interested in the same things, and our lives all revolve around the same person—Jesus Christ.

When the time came for me to leave, one of the women, a kindly looking lady named Ruth Seals, offered her home to us on our next trip to Philadelphia. And I once again praised God for how beautifully he provides for his children. He is so good and takes care of us so well!

Thursday we worked again at the Institutes with Tara, and Art gave us her new program which consisted of nearly all standing. We left in the late afternoon and flew to Chicago, where we had a full day of radio and television programs to do on Friday.

It was frosty cold in Chicago that night, and Tara and I were both hoping for snow. It was past nine when we checked into the Hyatt Regency in downtown Chicago, but Tara wasn't tired. She looked up at the bellman and batted her big gray eyes at him. "Do you think it might snow tonight?" she asked wistfully.

"I hope not!" came his reply. "Why? Do you want it to snow?"

"Oh, yes," Tara said. "I live in California, and it never snows there."

"Well," the bellman relented, "it might, but I doubt it. We haven't had much snow this year."

Tara sighed.

This dialog was repeated with the clerk behind the check-in desk. Then we went up to our room and began to get ready for bed. It wasn't long before the phone began ringing. "Mr. Nason? This is the bellman. Tell your little girl it's snowing outside!"

"Mr. Nason? This is the car attendant. Tell your daughter it's snowing!"

"Mr. Nason? This is the room clerk. It's snowing!"

We must have received five different calls from people who had heard that Tara wanted snow!

"Lord, who says people in big cities aren't friendly? Your love shining through the eyes of a little girl can touch the hearts of people anywhere!"

We threw our clothes back on and went out into the snowy night. It was so beautiful to see the snow glowing in the brightness around the streetlights. Tara was thrilled, and I was so glad that she was able to experience this snowfall firsthand.

The next morning it was still snowing lightly as we walked to WLS Television. We were to appear on "AM Chicago" with Steve Edwards and Sandy Freeman. I had been on several Los Angeles television programs since the book had come out, but I was still awfully nervous. My friend Mary Gail, herself an aspiring actress, says even the most famous of movie stars are usually nervous before appearing on camera, and that this is the mark of a good performer. I always try to remind myself of that fact when I'm fighting my own private case of stage fright. There is always so much I want to say, but all my life I have found it easier to write down important things than to say them out loud. As it turned out, Steve and Sandy were excellent hosts and asked such good questions that Mike and I both felt it was one of our very best television interviews.

The snow had turned to sleet outside, the wind was blowing, and it was bitter cold. But Tara and I loved it! We went high up in one of the skyscrapers to see Len Cohen and Herb Isaacs at Kelly, Scott, and Madison, an advertising agency Mike does business with in

Chicago. Tara and I thought it was fun to look out the windows at the stormy gray sky and see the tops of some of the taller buildings covered in mist.

Mike appeared on other programs during the day, and Tara and I just relaxed and watched. Late that afternoon we drove through the snowy suburbs to the airport, thankful to be going home again.

Tara's teacher, Carol Mogan, came to me one day shortly after our return. "I've tried every approach I know," she said, "but I just can't seem to teach Tara to read. I know she's a bright little girl, but I'm just not reaching her. I'd like to have the school district psychologist test Tara to see if they can help me find the key."

This only confirmed a fear I had had for several years. I had tried to push it as far back in my mind as possible, but every now and then it would raise its ugly head and make its presence known. I had tried to teach Tara to read almost constantly, beginning at age three. Glenn Doman, director of the Institutes, is a world authority on teaching young children to read, and reading is an integral part of the programs he gives to the brain-injured children in his care. But on his reading method, Tara and I were complete flops. I had wanted to believe it was my fault, that I just wasn't a good teacher. Surely, I had thought, when Tara is old enough and has a regular schoolteacher, she will learn readily.

I had even made excuses for Tara the previous year when, at age five, her homebound kindergarten teacher had been unable to make much headway. "She's only five," I had reasoned. "Next year she'll do better." But now Tara was nearly seven, and she had an excellent teacher who was applying a many-disciplined approach, and she still couldn't read.

Mrs. Mogan scheduled three sessions of testing with the school psychologists. We also arranged for vision and hearing evaluations. When all the screening had been completed, I wasn't really all that surprised about the findings.

"Tara is a severely brain-injured little girl," we were told, "and she functions remarkably well in the light of her many disabilities." That much we already knew and had been well aware of for nearly five years. We were told that Tara's hearing and auditory perception were excellent. This also came as no surprise.

Her spatial relations are fairly good, as is her long-term memory. Her short-term memory, however, has deficits, and she has difficulty performing under pressure. She may know someone very well, but if he comes up to her and asks, "Do you remember me? What's my name?" Tara will draw a complete blank and be unable to respond. This has hurt many people's feelings, making them think that Tara really doesn't remember them or care about them, when actually it is only Tara's memory that momentarily misfunctions.

But by far Tara's biggest stumblingblock on the road to reading is her faulty visual perception. She was cortically blind for several months following her accident, and even though the visual area in her brain regained its function somewhat, its interpretation of visual images is far from accurate. We just really don't know exactly what Tara sees. She doesn't always appear to see the same thing each time she looks at an object. She also isn't always able to transfer. She can learn a word on a flashcard and be unable to read it when it is printed on the page of a book. But then again, sometimes she *can* transfer. I looked at the report the pediatric ophthalmologist sent back to the school district, and all he would venture as a diagnosis was "possible cortical blindness." Actually, we know Tara isn't blind, but that's about all we really do know.

At any rate, after the test results were explained to us, it was easy to see why Tara was unable to read. After five years of struggling with Mark's learning disabilities, Mike and I at least understand that they have nothing to do with basic intelligence. I think that is one of the most frustrating things about being the parent of a child with learning problems. You can look at the child and know he is smart. And yet sometimes trying to teach him is rather like beating your head against a brick wall.

The thought of Tara having learning disabilities was devastating to me. "Why, Lord?" I wanted to ask. "Isn't it enough that Tara can't walk or use her hands? Is she also to be denied the pleasure of reading? Everyone else's children can learn how to read. Why can't mine? Why me, Lord? Why me?"

How easy it is to be bitter against God sometimes. How much like human nature to look for someone to blame, to nurse your hurts, to feel sorry for yourself. But does it ever really do any good? I don't think so.

I know Tara has learning disabilities. So what am I going to do about it? Shall I build myself a wall of hatred? Shall I dislike every child who can read? Shall I reject my own child because she can't? Or maybe I could spend all my time blaming myself and my husband and feeling guilty about it and playing the "maybe I should have done this" or "oh, I know I shouldn't have done that" game. All those methods of dealing with problems are guaranteed to make me totally ineffective.

Oh, I know I make mistakes sometimes. Doesn't everybody? But the biggest mistake of all is to so dwell on your mistakes that it kills your initiative. I thank God that my husband shares my positive attitude, and so together we forge ahead.

We have set as our goal that Tara, and in fact all the children, reach their maximum potential. And we're willing to try practically anything in an effort to speed them on their way. Consequently, we've gone up a lot of blind alleys. For some reason, the methods that work well for other children don't always work well for ours. But we keep hoping that someday, somehow, we'll hit upon the right combination of personalities, treatments, and methods that will work for our children.

Many people have been especially kind to our family, one of whom is a petite white-haired woman named Arla Johnson. She runs a vision development center in nearby Laguna Hills, which works with children who have learning disabilities. The approach there is similar to that of the Institutes in that they attempt to treat the problem, which is in the brain, rather than concentrate on the symptoms. They have many different ways of working through the visual pathways to the brain and have been quite successful in helping many children and adults as well.

Unfortunately, as is usually the case, vision therapy is quite expensive and is not covered by insurance. Mrs. Johnson was kind enough to share her love for God by treating Mark and Tara free of charges for over a year. These appointments twice a week further complicated our already full schedule, but Mike and I both felt it was well worth it. Thank the Lord for Terry, who often helped me out by driving the children back and forth when he himself wasn't in school.

April was a big month for us. Christa was turning two, and Tara was busy trying to toilet train her. We kept her potty chair in Tara's workroom, and Tara was dedicated and persistent. I may have had to train Tara twice, but I barely had to lift a finger with Christa. Tara did it all!

God was also busy getting all the right people together at just the right time to work two more very special miracles!

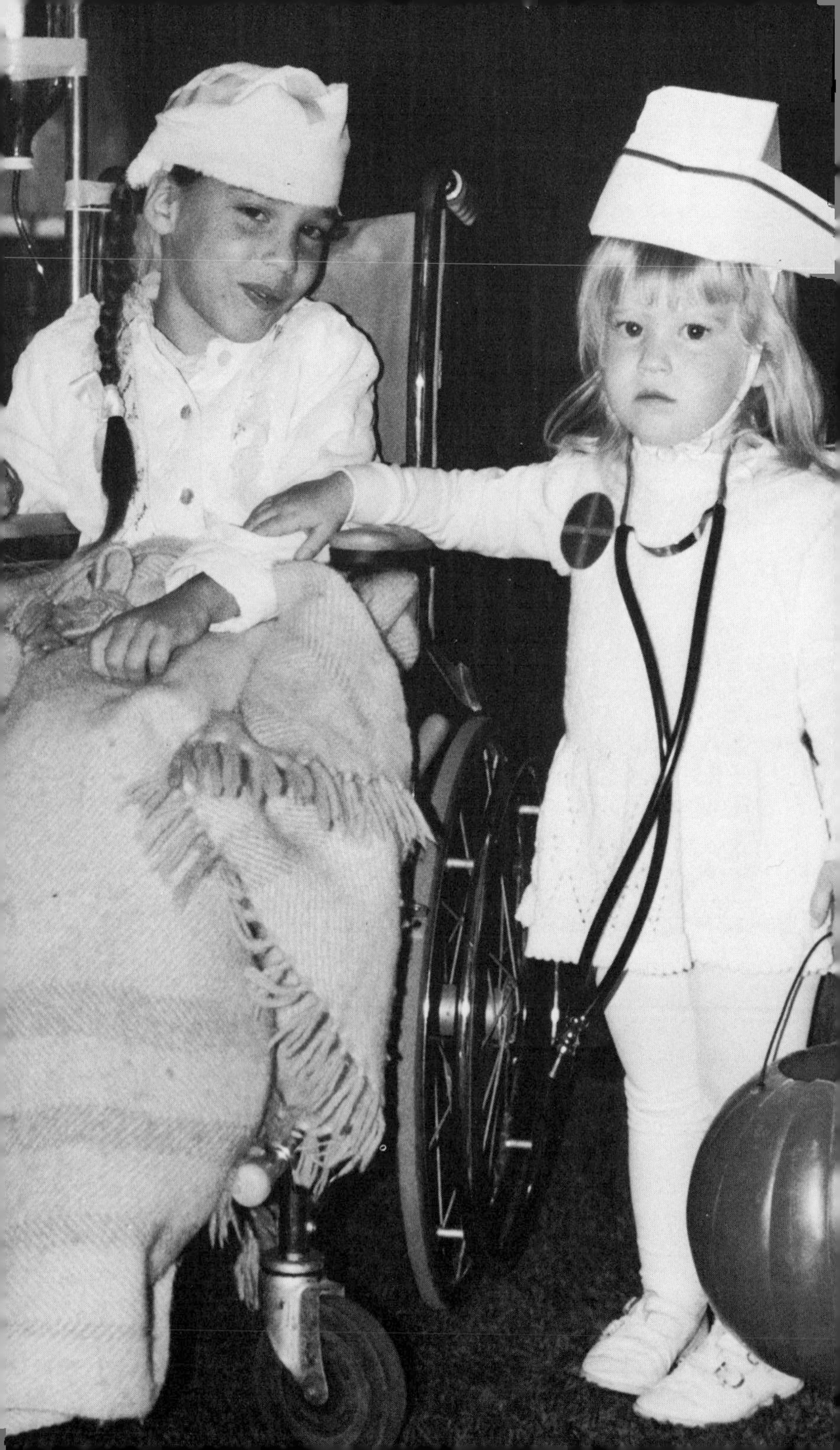

CHAPTER NINE
We See Miracles

My friend Mary Gail and her husband Bob Shutte were buying a home through a real estate agent. Mary Gail is so vivacious and so enthusiastic about Tara that she tells everyone she comes in contact with all about her. She had animatedly told her realtor, Linda Jackson, all about Tara and our family, and had even loaned her the book *Tara* to read.

Linda read the book and was very impressed by the story. I hesitate to call it *our* story, because it is really *God's* story—the story of the Holy Spirit working in and through a family. In God's providence, Linda was a friend of one of the executives of Family Films, makers of Christian movies which are shown in churches and schools.

She asked Mary Gail if she might let her friend read the book also. He liked the story so much that he was interested in making a documentary film about Tara. We were so thrilled when we received the phone call from Paul Kidd, Director of Product Development at Family Films. Imagine! Making a movie about us! This would be a way of reaching more people with the message of God's love.

Mike went up one day and met with Paul Kidd, Stan Hersh (the President of Family Films), Jim Lawrence (one of their producer-directors), and several other staff members. They discussed the business end of the film and came to an agreement on terms. But the most important part was yet to come. Would they like Tara? Would they think she could play herself in a movie?

I wasn't at all worried about Tara's ability to star in a movie. I knew she could do it! For myself, I had plenty of doubts. Me? Appear in a movie? How could I ever be so brave? I wondered. Jim Lawrence and Paul Kidd made an appointment to come over and meet Tara and watch her work. They didn't admit it, but I think they were expecting a depressing sight. People usually expect to be upset when they go to visit someone with brain injury.

They walked into Tara's workroom early one June morning and were met by one of her most radiant smiles. Tara loves to have new people come to visit her, especially men; and she really knows how to win hearts, as only little girls can. They watched her go through her program and even stayed for half of her school time as she worked with Mrs. Mogan.

While Tara was finishing her schooling, the two men came downstairs to chat with Mike and me about the kind of movie they were thinking of making about Tara. It would be a documentary based on the book, but not actually telling a story. They would not use actors; we would have to play our own parts. And they would film the movie here at our home as well as travel with us to Philadelphia. It sure sounded exciting!

Our conversation was cut short by loud sobs coming from Tara's workroom. She was crying as though her little heart were broken. Mrs. Mogan started down the stairs, and she too was crying. Then it dawned on me; this was the last day of school! Mrs. Mogan and Tara had spent nine months working closely together, and now student and teacher had to part.

I ran upstairs to comfort Tara and saw her lying on the floor on her back. Her little face was all screwed up as she sobbed, and the tears were flowing copiously. She feels everything so deeply, I thought, as I gathered her up into my arms. The eleven o'clock patterners came all too soon, and of necessity Tara had to dry her tears and get to work once more.

For the next few weeks I could think of only one thing: a movie was going to be filmed at my house, and I wanted it to be clean! Terry helped me, and one of my patterners, Pat Devereaux, watched the children for me. We scrubbed and polished every surface both seen and hidden. Of course, I knew they wouldn't be taking pictures of my closets, but I just wanted to be sure. That was one of the best spring cleanings my house has ever gotten!

Jim Lawrence made arrangements to bring a

cameraman and a soundman out the last weekend in June for filming. We had already planned to hold Tara's seventh birthday party that Saturday, and he was pleased at the prospect of including that also in the movie.

The Sunday before, Mike, Mark, Tara, and Christa were playing hide and seek while I was preparing dinner. Mark and Christa were darting back and forth, and the air was filled with shouts and giggles. Mike was partners with Tara, and he would roll her wheelchair to a good hiding place while the others counted.

Our home has a raised ceramic tile entrance hall with stepdowns into the living room and Mark's bedroom. Mark's room has double doors, and the tile extends a couple of feet beyond them before it steps down to a wood parquet. Mike thought this would be a super place to wheel Tara so she could hide from her brother and sister. He rolled her in, locked her brakes, shut the double doors, and sat down in a chair in the living room. Tara could hear Mark looking for her, and she got excited and began kicking her legs and waving her arms. She accidentally unlocked the brakes so that there was nothing to prevent the chair from rolling. Her kicking caused her wheelchair to roll ahead, falling forward off the edge of the tile and onto the wooden floor.

Tara, who was strapped into the chair, was helpless to protect herself. She let out a blood-curdling shriek as she catapulted face first onto the hard floor. Christa was frightened by Tara's screams and came out of her hiding place, running for her daddy. At the same time,

Mike leaped from his chair and dashed across the entrance hall toward Mark's bedroom. Christa got in his way, and in his eagerness he accidentally knocked her down, chipping her front teeth.

Tara was lying face down on the floor, still strapped in her wheelchair. Her knees were skinned, and her face was bruised and bleeding. To our horror, we saw that she had knocked out both her two front teeth and several others were loose. It took us quite a while to get her to calm down and stop crying, and then we took her down the street to our pediatrician's house for him to take a look at her. Thank God, she was shaken up, but nothing more.

The next day, after we had all recuperated from the mishap, Mike and I began to worry about what Jim Lawrence would say. He had seen a beautiful little girl with perfect white teeth who was going to star in his movie. What would he think when he saw two gaping holes where her teeth had been? Maybe he wouldn't want to make the movie after all.

Mike phoned Jim and explained the accident to him, telling him of his star's missing teeth. But instead of being upset, Jim was delighted. "Few things make a child so appealing as missing front teeth," he explained with a laugh. "I bet she's cuter than ever."

By Thursday night my house was clean, and Tara's bruises had healed. Around 5:00 a van pulled into our driveway, absolutely loaded with filmmaking equipment. Lights, cameras, dollies, wires, and cable were all unloaded and stored in our garage. I hadn't realized it took so many things to make a movie.

Jim, Bob Ebinger (the cameraman), and Ron Kaufman (the soundman) went over our house carefully, deciding which pieces of equipment they would need in each location. They wanted to get an early start on Friday morning and tried to set up as many things as possible that evening. They had to run cables up the side of the house and through windows in the workroom. Then they gelled the workroom windows, putting a light brown cellophane-type material on them to help achieve a better lighting situation in the room. Somehow during the process, Jim Lawrence put his hand through the window pane, breaking the glass. We were so thankful that he wasn't badly hurt. Finally everything was in readiness. The film crew went back to their motel, and the Nason family was left wondering excitedly what the morrow would bring.

That Friday morning dawned hot and dry. It was the real beginning of our hot summer weather for the year. Mission Viejo, although it is only ten miles inland from the Pacific Ocean, is separated from the sea breezes by the hills. In the summer, when it never rains, its air is dry and hot like the desert, and the thermometer lingers around ninety degrees for weeks. Our home, thank the Lord, is air-conditioned so that we pass the summer in comfort. However, on this particular hot summer day, Jim Lawrence explained to us that we would not be able to run our air-conditioner. The noise would interfere with their sound system. Also, their equipment would be using so much electricity that the circuits would not be able to handle the additional drag the air-conditioner would make.

Tara's program requires the expenditure of so much energy that we had never even attempted to work her during those few times when for some reason our air-conditioner was not working. It was just too hot to even consider putting forth that much effort. But now we were being asked to work all day long in 100-degree weather in what is normally the hottest room of our house, under the additional glare and heat of movie lights. And at the same time we had to try to look calm, cool, and collected!

I didn't think we would ever make it, but we did. And besides that, it was fun! Tara was a real trouper and did her best to please; and all the patterners were wonderful, doing things over and over without complaining. I was kept busy running up and down the stairs with pitchers of ice water for everyone and handing out towels to mop damp faces before pictures were taken.

It was without a doubt the hottest, hardest pattern day we've ever had, but also one of the most rewarding. As the lights blazed and the cameras whirred, we each realized the wonderful opportunity God had given us to give the world a glimpse of what it is like to be brain-injured and to show people God's grace which is freely given to all who ask.

They interviewed Terry that afternoon and gave him a chance to talk about his new friendship with Christ and what it had meant in his life. It made me so very thankful to God that he had let me share in this dramatic conversion.

As evening drew near and the day's therapy came to a close, the film crew was busy moving its base of operations to the living room. It was fascinating to watch them set up lights outside the windows so as to give the impression of moonlight. We had asked three of our longstanding faithful patterners to come over and be filmed. Each had graciously accepted, and Eleanor Lau, Margo Clarke, and Corinne Pyle spent hours in the heat sharing the things they had seen Christ doing in and through our family. What a thrill it was to see God glorified in such a beautiful way!

The next morning was so exciting and hectic as I prepared for Tara's seventh birthday party. The film crew went out into the backyard and took some shots of Tara, Mike, and Christa playing with our dog Muffet. The little girls began arriving for the birthday party around 2:00, each one dressed in ruffles and curls.

Tara wore a beautiful red-and-white-checked dress with a white organdy pinafore. It had been Mary Gail's dress as a child, and Tara had worn it when she had been the flower girl in Mary Gail and Bob's wedding. I braided her hair and then looped her braids and tied red-and-white-checked bows on the loops. Little Christa wore a yellow dress with a white dotted-swiss pinafore. At first Mark didn't want to come to the party. "It's just for girls," he had scoffed. But as the festivities got under way, his enthusiasm got the best of him. He went to his room and put on a pair of brown pants and a brown Hawaiian shirt and came back outside to join in the fun.

It was so hot out there, and even with all that sunshine the film crew had their lights going. But the children didn't seem to mind or even to notice that they were being immortalized on film. The girls helped Tara open her packages and even sang Happy Birthday twice at the request of Jim Lawrence. Everyone, including the film crew and their wives, had ice cream and cake; and a good time was had by all, especially Tara.

I am usually exhausted after giving a birthday party. There is something about the excitement of the day and the challenge of entertaining several small children that is just guaranteed to wear me out. I generally plan nothing else for the day and concentrate on recuperating, but this time such a luxury was not possible. I was more keyed up after the party than I had been beforehand.

That night after dinner was Mike's and my time to be filmed for the movie. I had thought they would ask me questions that I could answer. I am quite comfortable in interview situations, so I wasn't too worried. However, as it turned out, that is not what they had in mind.

In the first place, in that sweltering heat they built a fire in the fireplace and pushed the couch right next to it. Then they sat me on the couch and turned the lights on. "Just gaze into the fire and look melancholy like you're deep in thoughts of the past," Jim said. "Then just start talking about Tara."

"Just start talking!" I sputtered. "You mean you're not going to ask me questions?" No, they were not going to interview me. They wanted me to speak from the heart, and I was mortified. "Lord," I complained, "I know I told you I'd do anything for you, but this is ridiculous! How much do you expect one shy woman to do anyway? Lord, you know that on my own strength this would be impossible for me to accomplish. I'm trusting you to speak for me, by the power of your Holy Spirit."

My grace is sufficient for you, for power is perfected in weakness (2 Corinthians 12:9).

I asked God to glorify himself through me, and he didn't let me down. I spent two hours talking, and when I was through I knew I had done a good job. The other day a man came up to me and said, "You look good on film, but you're beautiful in person!" At first I couldn't figure out what he was talking about, and then it dawned on me.

"The movie!" I exclaimed. "You saw me in our movie. Didn't I look terrible? They made me keep my eyes partially closed and kept the camera on my worst side."

"Never mind about that," he replied. "Your witness was just perfect!"

He couldn't have said anything that would have pleased me more. And I know I wasn't the one who did it; it was God working through me. I love him so much!

Mike, of course, did an excellent job with no

trouble at all. He is such an extrovert and such a good speaker, and his part-time announcing on Hour of Power has helped him not to be camera shy. It took us all until way past midnight to finish the day's shooting. I sure did sleep well that night!

The following morning, the film crew went with us to church. They stayed with Tara and Mark in their Sunday school class and got shots of all the children singing. Then they packed up and went home.

We didn't see them again until early September. They met us at the airport as we were all preparing to fly back to Philadelphia for Tara's five-day evaluation at the Institutes. They planned to do some filming on the plane, and I was wondering how my part of it would turn out. I was two months pregnant with Shannon and had terrible nausea in addition to my usual fear of airplanes; I wasn't quite sure how the combination would affect me. However, things all worked out fairly well, and we landed safely in Philadelphia after a smooth flight.

Praise God, another one of my prayers was answered. The weather was cool, not hot and humid, as Philadelphia can often be in September. Ruth Seals, whom I had met at the Murrays' the previous February, welcomed us warmly into her home. Her husband Fred, a mechanic for TWA, also did his best to make us feel wanted. Tara, whom they had never met, didn't take long to find a special place in their hearts.

Jim, Bob, and Ron followed us all around the Institutes that week, filming everything. It was so thrilling to have some of our favorite people captured on film, especially Glenn Doman and Art Sandler.

Art was ecstatic over a new piece of equipment he had invented which he called a Spring Turtle. It consisted of a track on the ceiling from which a frame and a harness were suspended by ropes and springs. Tara was placed in the harness in a hands and knees position, and the ropes were adjusted so that her hands and knees just touched the floor. The supports and springs created a sort of weightless condition for Tara in which she had more freedom of movement than normal. Gravity is the natural enemy of children like Tara, and the Spring Turtle in some respects eliminated a lot of the gravitational force on her.

We were all elated to see Tara begin to creep on her hands and knees in a cross pattern across the floor in the Turtle. Nothing we had ever tried for her had allowed her to move so freely. We knew before we were told that this would be an important part of Tara's new program. The fact that Tara was creeping in pattern also indicated that all the patterns we had given her were actually making an impression on her brain. For four years we had been putting information into her "computer." The Spring Turtle enabled her to put out in performance some of what had been going in.

In all, it was an excellent visit. Tara received a good report, and the filming went well. We came home enthusiastic about Tara's new program, and Jim Lawrence came home enthusiastic about the movie.

The filming was complete, all 6,400 feet of it. Mike and I wondered how on earth they could possibly edit ten hours of film down to a thirty-five-minute movie. It took them several months, but they finally completed the task.

Dr. Schuller was so excited over the movie that he decided to hold the world premiere of it right there at Garden Grove Community Church. It was scheduled for March 29, and I was nervous. My baby was due April 5 and I was usually early. What if I was in the hospital during the premiere of my own movie?

Shannon was very cooperative, making his appearance March 12. His life was out of danger by the twentieth, and our entire family was so jubilant and so full of praise for the Lord that the first showing of our movie seemed a perfect way to end such a faith-testing, faith-building month.

Dr. Schuller, who always does things in such a big way, advertised the movie heavily in all the local newspapers. Even so, Mike and I didn't really know quite what to expect in the way of a turnout. As the big evening approached, we began to get more and more nervous. Neither one of us had seen the film, and we were both apprehensive as to how each family member might look and sound. "What if nobody comes? What if nobody likes it?" we worried.

March 29 finally arrived, and as we were driving up to the church with the Patanés, my stomach was turning flipflops. When we got to the church, my heart nearly stopped. I had rarely seen the parking lot so full. People were everywhere! Sitting on the floor, standing in the aisles, and still streaming in. The sanctuary seats 1,700 people, and there were over 2,000 crammed in there that night.

I was totally astonished. Never in my wildest dreams had I imagined a turnout like that! It was downright embarrassing and made us even more worried as to whether or not people would like the movie.

The lights dimmed, and a picture of an airplane being serviced for takeoff appeared on the screen accompanied by strains from Mozart. As the plane soared into the sky, superimposed over it were the words "Family Films presents TARA." Even though I should have been expecting it, the words sent a shock right through me, and I was flooded with the realization of the wonderful miracle God had performed. To think that he could use someone as everyday as me, a family as ordinary as ours, to do something so beautiful. "O God!" I wanted to shout. "I am so unworthy! To you goes all the glory!"

The thirty-five minutes sped quickly by, and the audience laughed with us and cried with us. When the movie was over, there was a dead silence for nearly a minute. This happens, I am told, every time our movie is shown. I don't think people know exactly what to do. But in the end, they gave the film a rousing standing ovation. Mike and I were both moved to tears, it was such a precious moment. Dr. Schuller had an altar call, and I was able to see that the Lord had used our story to touch hearts and lead people to Christ. And I cried out silently to God, "It was worth it all! It was worth it all!"

The next week the church advertised the movie again and another large crowd came to see it. Since then it has been shown in churches and schools all over the country to the glory of God's holy name. How thankful we all are to have been a part of something so wondrously special!

Way back in April, when we were still in the talking stages of our movie, God was busy putting together another series of miracles that would affect our family. Four times a year, Dr. Schuller holds an Institute for Successful Church Leadership there on the grounds of Garden Grove Community Church. Only a few days before the April Institute was to begin, its director, Wilbert Eichenberger, received a phone call from Harold Maiden, pastor of Griffith Methodist Church in Las Vegas. Pastor Maiden, who was anxious to attend the Institute, was told that the enrollment was full. Would he like to come to the next Institute, to be held in July?

The pastor then explained that he was desperate; he was even thinking of giving up the ministry. July might be too late. Because of the urgency of his situation, Dr. Schuller said he could squeeze in one more person, and Pastor Maiden was able to attend.

During his time at the Institute, Harold Maiden had his love for God quickened and his faith strengthened. He made a new commitment to Christ and returned to Las Vegas with a new zeal for his church. He also bought several books at the Institute which he took home to read. One of these was the book *Tara*.

Griffith Methodist Church runs a preschool,

and one of the children who was attending at that time was a beautiful little five-year-old girl named Alisa Goldstein. She was the young daughter of a Jewish couple, Mort and Dolores.

On June 20, 1975, Alisa was hit by a car in the street in front of her home. She received serious injury to her brain and went immediately into a coma. Her parents were heartbroken, and her father particularly was experiencing great difficulty in coping with the tragedy.

Pastor Maiden, having just read *Tara*, felt that perhaps here was a book that could be of help to the Goldsteins. He went and visited little Alisa in the hospital, saw her lovely face silent and unknowing, saw her once-healthy body still and stiff. He spoke to her parents and left them *Tara* to read. Then he called Mike at the church to see if he would mind calling the Goldsteins. Perhaps he might have an encouraging word for them.

Mike and I look upon this type of counseling as a very special ministry that God has given us. We know so well the pain and confusion, the utter helplessness that parents feel when their child has been recently brain-injured. And because we have been there ourselves, we are in a unique position to help the family as few others can.

We can offer advice for treatment or therapy, and give practical suggestions. But especially we can give hope, and we can show empathy because we know how they feel. We can assure the parents that they can live through and overcome tragedy, and we can urge them not to give up on their child just because the doctors have. We can also explain to the family what we have found to be the key to overcoming life's hurts—the person of Jesus Christ.

It was, therefore, with great joy that Mike called the Goldsteins; joy because he knew he could be of help to them. He spoke with both Mort and Dolores, encouraging them to hold firm their faith in their daughter and in their God. He left them our phone number, telling them to get in touch with us whenever they needed help.

This was standard procedure for us in cases of this sort, and we always counted it a real blessing when parents called us back just to talk or to ask for advice; but this time Mike just couldn't get the Goldsteins out of his mind. He could barely concentrate on his work, because vague worries about this family would keep cropping up at the most inopportune times.

For over two weeks, he kept hearing God's call. "Go to them!" he seemed to say. "All the way to Las Vegas?" Mike would query back time after time. Finally he could stand it no longer. "Donna," he said over the phone early one afternoon, "I won't be home for dinner tonight. I'm flying to Las Vegas. I don't know why, but I've just got to go. The Lord wants me to. I'm going to take the 2:00 flight from Orange County Airport, spend some time with the Goldsteins, and come home on the 8:00 plane."

Mort met Mike at the airport, and the two men embraced. There was an immediate affinity between them. They drove straight to the hospital where Dolores was waiting with little Alisa, who lay still, looking as though she were in pain. To Mike this was not an unusual sight; Alisa wasn't the first little girl he had seen in such a tragic condition.

He was able to share some of our experiences with Tara, and to give some insights as to what might or might not be going on in Alisa's brain. At last, the distraught parents thought, here is someone who understands. They plied Mike with questions about Tara and all the various things we have done for her. Mike had taken for them a recent picture of Tara, grinning happily at her birthday party, so they could see concrete evidence that their daughter had hopes of coming out of her vegetative state.

But most of all, Mike was able to tell them about our best friend, their Messiah, the Lord Jesus Christ. "It is he who sent me to you," Mike asserted, knowing without a shadow of doubt that he spoke the truth. And this dear Jewish couple believed Mike. Dolores had other friends who had been telling her they had found their Messiah in the person of Jesus, and she was very interested.

This was the first time since Alisa's tragic accident that Mort had been able to open up and share his feelings and frustrations and fears. He was finally able to let off steam and get his emotions out into the open. And he was convinced that God did love him, and that he hadn't abandoned him in his grief. Since Alisa's accident, Mort had been in a very serious state of depression which had been growing steadily worse. On this particular day, he had reached his wit's end. Only God knows what might have happened to him had Mike not paid him a visit and loved him for Christ.

Mike came home that night praising God for not letting up on him until he had done what he asked. He still maintains that he has never felt more in tune with God than he did that fateful night, and it stands out as one of Mike's great spiritual experiences.

We kept in close contact with the Goldsteins during Alisa's two-and-a-half-month hospital stay, and helped them plan how they would bring her home. That fall, shortly after Alisa's homecoming, Mort and Dolores flew into Orange County to visit us for the weekend. I was so excited to meet this couple whom God obviously loved so much.

We had previously agreed for Tara to be a guest on a children's version of "Praise the Lord Program" at our local Christian television station, Channel 40, on that particular Saturday afternoon. Mike and I hoped that the Goldsteins wouldn't mind spending two hours of their "get away from it all" weekend in a TV studio.

But it appeared that the Lord had set it up that way on purpose. Mort and Dolores had such a great spiritual hunger that they literally gobbled up everything that was presented on Channel 40 that day. They loved the music and the prayers and the words of praise. Both of them sat transfixed throughout the entire program, tears flowing down their cheeks.

The next morning we took them to church with us. Mike was busy at work with the videotaping of the service, so Mort, Dolores (whom I now called Dee), Terry, and I sat together in a front pew. Dee sat next to me, and she grabbed my hand during the opening hymn and squeezed it hard. Both she and Mort were again in tears throughout the hour. It has been my experience that such a thorough cleansing through tears is often the ministry of the Holy Spirit, and I really felt his presence so strongly that morning.

When church was over, Mike arranged for them to go into Dr. Schuller's study and speak with him before their return to Las Vegas. We waited out in the car for quite a long time, curious about what was happening to the Goldsteins. Finally Dr. Schuller walked them out to the parking lot. They each embraced him warmly, and I could see they had been crying again.

"Here are two people who have just had a personal confrontation with their Messiah, Jesus," Dr. Schuller said in a tone of quiet joy. And oh, the joy that touched my soul at that moment! I knew that with Jesus living in their hearts, this precious couple would be prepared to meet the upcoming challenges of caring for their daughter. Jesus would see them through. I knew it! No matter how rough the road, they would make it to the end.

Little Alisa, who is now six-and-a-half years old, has had a really remarkable recovery. She can walk and run and play. She likes music, and she can learn, although she has some learning disabilities as Tara does. She is hyperactive, but then so are a lot of other children who have not been hit by cars. She is a beautiful human being with a special place in God's heart, and we are thankful he let us play a part in her story. Mort, Dolores, Alisa, and her fifteen-year-old sister, Laurie, all know Jesus as their Messiah because Michael cared enough to obey God's call.

The Goldstein family are among the many people that have touched our lives. A few years ago Mike was appointed a member of the Fairview State Hospital Advisory Board by Governor Reagan. This five-man board oversees programs and procedures of the hospital, which houses 1,700 developmentally disabled clients from all over California, and reports to the governor and the state legislature. Mike and I consider this a wonderful opportunity for him to offer his unique vantage point, both as a Christian and as a father of a brain-injured child, within the vast arena of state institutions. Mike was recently elected chairman of this important board, and we know God has great plans in store.

Then there was the time a few years ago when a local fifteen-year-old-boy accidentally hanged himself. He was without oxygen to his brain and received massive brain damage. After spending several weeks in coma, the boy was released from the hospital and admitted to a convalescent home where he would presumably spend the rest of his life in a semiconscious state while being cared for by the staff.

It was a terribly expensive place, and the boy's aunt wrote a letter to the Troubleshooter column of the Santa Ana *Register*, asking for donations to help his parents with the mounting medical bills. The Troubleshooter passed the letter on to us, and Mike called the parents and gave them an alternative nobody else had suggested. Why not bring Scott home and care for him? Home care is free, and if Scott could improve, home is where it could happen best.

Merle and Susie Perkins did bring Scott home and began taking him to the Institutes in Philadelphia for treatment. It's been a long, hard battle; and it's not over yet. But Scott is now nineteen years old, and he can walk and talk and drive a car. He graduated from high school and is now attending a college for learning disabled young adults in Philadelphia.

His parents are active in High Hopes Neurological Recovery Group, an organization founded by Lee Merryman of Newport Beach. Her handsome fifteen-and-a-half-year-old son, Mike, was brain-injured in a motorcycle accident just after Christmas in January 1972. I read about him in the newspaper and called to give Lee what encouragement I could.

Devout Christians, the Merrymans, like the Perkinses, have devoted years to helping Mike live up to his full God-given potential. And like Scott, Mike also walks and talks. So great has been his courage that when he walked forward to receive his high school diploma, his classmates gave him a standing ovation. He is now attending Orange Coast College.

I had had no personal contact with Lee since the time of Mike's accident, but she had kept abreast of Tara's progress through different newspaper articles and was aware that we had written a book about her. So burdened was her family with Mike's medical expenses that Lee couldn't afford to buy the book *Tara*, which she was so anxious to read.

Then one day the woman who had been Mike's nurse in the intensive care ward during his hospital stay, herself a Christian, came by and brought Lee a gift—*Tara*! Lee sat down to read the book and didn't get up until she had finished it. As she lived through our experiences with Tara, she relived her own experiences with Mike. "The Nasons went through it too! They understand!" The floodgates flew open! Lee wept. And those tears washed away years of negative emotions that had been hidden so deep inside.

Lee couldn't sleep that night; she was actually travailing, giving birth to a dream. She was filled with a burning desire to help Mike and the many other local teenagers who have been brain-injured in accidents.

She conceived the plan of forming a group in which parents of these children could lend each other moral support and help each other with mutual problems. She also envisioned a group of parents who would be willing to go to the hospitals and counsel with parents of children just recently injured.

Her dream also included activities for these young people—ways that they could come together for fellowship and recreation. Too often they are misfits, left out of the mainstream of life where they had previously functioned so well. They become friendless, despondent. She thought of an organization of peers, in which they could make friends and feel at home. She also wanted to provide educational, vocational, and career training for these teenagers. She wanted to help them reach their full potential.

In the two-and-one-half years since the inception of her idea, the Merrymans, the Perkinses, and other dedicated parents like them have worked night and day to make their dream a reality. We are so very thankful that God used Tara's story as a catalyst for this outstanding work.

There are countless others whom I have never met. Distraught voices over the telephone, tear-stained letters. People hurting and searching and crying out for help. "Help me! Somebody please help me!" I'm not a doctor and I don't have any miracle cure for brain-injury. I wish I did! But I'm a mother who knows what it feels like to hurt, and I can pass on the knowledge it's taken me years to acquire. I can be a listening ear and a shoulder to cry on. I can love these people in Jesus' name.

CHAPTER TEN
New Perspectives

The summer when Tara was seven years old, Mike and I, both individually and collectively, did a lot of thinking and praying about her future. She had been hurt for five years, and while she had made enormous strides during that time she still had a very long way to go, especially in the area of mobility.

We had been patterning her for four years. Aside from her learning disabilities, she was normal emotionally and intellectually and her speech was good. But physically, although progress had undeniably been made, there was still very little she could do: crawl across the floor on her tummy, sit up, sometimes pick things up with her stiff little hands, provided the object was placed in just the right spot and she had plenty of time for lots of tries.

Realistically, we had to admit, if she continued to progress at her current rate, she would be an old woman before she could walk.

Did we really want to spend the next forty years of our lives cooped up in Tara's workroom eight hours a day, seven days a week? Suppose we did. Suppose we worked with Tara constantly for forty more years, so that at age forty-seven she was able to walk. What kind of a person would she be?

We thought about this very, very carefully, and we decided that she would probably be an emotionally and socially immature and maladjusted person. She would not have the wealth of knowledge a person of that age should have, because she would not have gone to school. She would not be able to relate to her peers, because she would never have had the chance to mingle with them. She would have no skills, because we would have been so busy trying to teach her to walk that she would not have had time to acquire any. Therefore, she would be unable to support herself. She might be able to walk, but she would still be dependent on us. She would not be a well-rounded person.

This, we decided, was definitely not what we wanted for our Tara. We had agreed at the beginning that we wanted her to reach her maximum potential. Spending forty years in a workroom didn't seem to be the way to bring about the desired result. In our opinion, the patterning therapy was the very best therapy we could give Tara. If there was ever a way to help her walk, patterning would have to be it. We knew we didn't want to stop.

What, then, could we do? We really prayed about it and felt that God gave us the answer upon which we both agreed. In Dana Point, an oceanside community some eighteen miles from our home, the school district had just completed construction of a beautiful school for the orthopedically and multiply-handicapped. They had traveled all over the state looking at schools of this type, and had tried to combine the best of what they saw into this structure.

It had big, airy classrooms with the latest in teaching aids, each one equipped with a full kitchen built to the wheelchair height of the students. It had a heated indoor swimming pool with facilities for each child to have swimming lessons twice a week. And most important, it had a staff of bright, young, enthusiastic, well-qualified teachers.

Mike and I both felt that the Lord wanted Tara in school. If only there were enough time for Tara to put in a full day at school and still have eight hours of patterning. That, we thought, would be ideal. Unfortunately, as is always the case in this world, we had to settle for less-than-perfect situation.

So, with considerable trepidation, we enrolled Tara in school, to begin September 1975. Classes were held from 8:30 to 2:00, but we withdrew Tara at 1:00 each day so she could fit in more hours of her program at home. She would be working from 1:30 to 5:30 each day, which meant that as soon as the bus dropped her off I would hurriedly put a body suit on her and take her upstairs to her workroom to begin her patterning.

This was to be our schedule on every day but Wednesday. One day during the summer I had been in the drugstore with all the children. A beautiful brunette came over to us and asked, "Is this Tara?" I, of course, replied that this was indeed Tara and that I was her mother.

"I've been wanting to get in touch with you," she said, after introducing herself as Nancy Clark. "I lead my daughter's group of Blue Birds, and we would just love to have Tara join our troop if you think she would enjoy it."

I couldn't have been more delighted! For Tara to be a member of a group such as this, for her to have the experience of mingling with normal girls her own age, to have the fun of crafts and field trips, was more wonderful than anything I could have thought of.

On Wednesdays Tara wore her red-and-blue Blue Bird uniform to school. She patterned from 1:30 to 3:00, and then attended her meeting from 3:30 to 4:45, returning home to pattern again from 5:00 to 6:00. It was a hectic day, but it meant so much to Tara.

Little Christa, my baby, was going to preschool on Tuesday and Thursday mornings, and oh, how she loved it! At two and a half she was learning so many wonderful things about the big, exciting world. And it was so thrilling for me to watch her progress and growth.

Tara, who had been fighting tonsillitis since age two, was finally going to have her tonsils taken out in October. I was as nervous as if she were undergoing brain surgery! Knowing how nauseated she gets after general anesthetic, I just kept worrying about her vomiting and irritating the surgical wounds in her throat. I had been through a tonsillectomy with Mark, and I knew it was no picnic. It's funny, but when Mark had had his tonsils out I had been pregnant with Christa, and now here I was pregnant again.

I wanted to spend the night with Tara in the hospital after her surgery, because I was terrified that she would get sick during the night, be unable to call a nurse, and choke to death on her own vomit. I was told that overnight stays were against hospital regulations, but that Tara could have a full-time special nurse to stay with her constantly. Knowing that a nurse would be with her really made me feel so much better. Also, we called in a prayer request to Channel 40's "PTL Program," and I knew all the prayer partners would be praying.

Tara came through the surgery with flying colors, recuperating quickly, as children usually do. While in the hospital, she received a darling flower arrangement with a card signed "Matthew Teddy Bear." During the summer, we had taken our favorite vacation, a week's stay at family camp at Forest Home Christian Conference Center. The Family Hour speaker was Norman Wright, a dynamic author, lecturer, and family counselor. We enjoyed so very much getting to know him and his family. His son Matthew, who is around Tara's age, is also brain-injured. Tara had loved him and always called him Teddy Bear. How thoughtful it was for the Wright family to send Tara flowers. With their busy schedule, they had remembered, and it meant so much to us.

Halloween was fast approaching, and I was

excited as always about costumes. Mark has been a monster for years on Halloween. He picks out the most gruesome mask he can find, wears his oldest, most ragged clothes, and splashes vampire blood all over himself. But with the girls, I can use my imagination and have fun doing something unique.

This year I decided to let Tara be an accident victim. After all, she had to go trick-or-treating in her wheelchair anyway, so I figured we could make the best of it and use it as a prop. We wrapped her head up in gauze, put her in pajamas, robe, and slippers, and attached an authentic-looking IV bottle to her wheelchair. Actually, it was made from an empty bottle of Hawaiian Punch. Of course, with her bright eyes and saucy smile, I didn't think she could really fool anyone.

Christa was to be her nurse, so we dressed her all in white. Terry made her a nurse's hat and badge, and she wore a stethoscope around her neck. They both looked so cute as we enthusiastically set out to conquer the neighborhood. I had to laugh in surprise when several of the neighbors drew me aside and whispered in furtive tone, "What happened to Tara? Did she take a turn for the worse?"

All during this time, we were beginning to note subtle changes in Tara. She loved school. She loved her teacher Maxine and all her classmates; she loved the learning and the art and the music. Her mind was being stimulated, and her horizons were broadening. She was discovering that she was an individual, a separate entity from everybody else.

Unfortunately, she had also learned that she was the only one in her class who had to work all afternoon. The other children could play, watch television, draw, go places. In short, they were all doing the kinds of things that she wanted to do but couldn't because of her patterning program.

This, Mike and I realized, was one of the reasons why Glenn Doman is so dead-set against the children on his program going to school. It was easy to see that school took Tara's mind off her therapy and made her less cooperative. In addition, the teachers there did not have the goal of normalcy for Tara that we have. They wanted to teach her to live with her handicap, to be happy in her wheelchair. They filled her mind with ideas such as, "When you are grown up, you can be a secretary in your wheelchair."

And so began the struggle of ideologies. It is so very difficult to know where to draw the line! If Tara is going to have to spend the rest of her life in a wheelchair, then I certainly want her to be happy and fulfilled and independent in it. But on the other hand, I don't want her to resign herself to being in a wheelchair as a permanent fact of life. To do so would be to stop trying. She's got to have a goal, and Mike and I both agree that any goal of less than perfect wholeness is unworthy. That doesn't necessarily mean that we expect Tara to reach that goal, but certainly the higher the goal, the higher the achievement will be. For Tara to set as her goal to spend her life in a wheelchair is easy; obviously that goal can be met. We feel that we must keep expanding her outlook as to what she can do.

Trying to keep on an even keel in this situation can be extremely difficult. We can't promise Tara that if she patterns and works hard every day, she will be well. Yet we must be encouraging her constantly not to settle for less than she can be.

In the end, the goals must be Tara's. She must learn to sift through all the alternatives and come up with the game plan she thinks is best for her life, just like all the children who are not in wheelchairs. And isn't that what growing up is all about? As parents we can teach and encourage and prod, but on the bottom line must go the child's own signature.

One Tuesday in February, Mike called me on the phone from his office. "Pack your bags and find sitters for the kids," he shouted enthusiastically. "I'm taking you to Hawaii for five days, and we're leaving Thursday morning."

"Thursday morning?" I repeated breathlessly. "That's the day after tomorrow! Have you forgotten that I am expecting a baby in five weeks?"

"No problem," Mike replied. "I already called the doctor. You can go; he says they have excellent doctors in Hawaii."

As I hung up the phone and sat in a daze at the kitchen table, I couldn't help thinking how very typical this episode was for my husband. And I knew he meant business, too! There was nothing for me to do but get on the telephone and begin making arrangements.

Terry, bless his heart, would stay with the

children. I always know he will take as good care of them as I do. And not only that, he always has my house sparkling clean when I return! That's a hard combination to beat. All my patterners agreed to carry on with Tara's therapy in my absence. What wonderful friends these women are!

When I started thinking about packing my bag, I realized I had a problem. I had no summer maternity clothes. I had to borrow some from one of our friends, Pat Devereaux. So with four sleeveless maternity dresses and much trembling, I took off in flight across the blue Pacific.

The Schullers and their four daughters flew with us. Actually, it was sort of a combination business-pleasure trip for Dr. Schuller and Mike, but it was pure pleasure for me. I had come almost all the way through an extremely miserable pregnancy while caring for three children, patterning Tara, and single-handedly doing laundry and cleaning for a 3000-square-foot house. In short, I was totally exhausted, mentally and physically.

To sleep late, dress leisurely, and eat breakfast in the beachside coffee shop while little birds flew in and out was like heaven to me. I sunbathed and read for hours, and napped in the afternoons. I made quite a spectacle on the beach. When I sank down into the sand, on my back, my pregnant stomach seemed to loom way into the sky. "That's OK," quipped Dr. Schuller, "it matches all the Hawaiian fruit. It's the symbol of a fruitful marriage."

That trip was something that seemed very

impractical, and if Mike had asked me if I had wanted to go (which he didn't—he never does!), I would have said an emphatic "No!" And yet it was very good for me, and something the Lord knew I needed before I went through the trauma of Shannon's early birth and subsequent difficulties. I returned home refreshed in body and spirit, and loaded down with pineapples, leis, and little girls' Hawaiian dresses.

Something else we especially enjoyed that spring was my brother's four-month stay in San Diego. Doug is radioman on a fast attack nuclear submarine stationed out of Connecticut. Living at opposite ends of the country, we don't get to see each other very often. He was attending a special computer school in San Diego, which is only an hour away from our home, and he often came up to spend his weekends with us. The children all adored their uncle, who was so good to spend time with them and play his guitar and sing for them. Christa was never able to manage saying Uncle Doug, so she called him Donald Duck, to everyone's amusement.

Just two days before Shannon was born, we had a visit from a delightful woman who has spent most of her adult life working in Childhood Evangelism. Shirley Wisner is now one of the leaders of this wonderful group which works so hard to spread the gospel of Christ to children around the world. She travels a good part of the year all over our country, lecturing and teaching people how best to reach young children with the message of salvation in Jesus.

Aunt Shirley, as she likes the children to call her, first heard me speak before the Teen Challenge women in Orange, and subsequently read our book *Tara*. She was especially touched by the fact that all our children came to know Jesus at a very early age, and that it was Mark who led Tara to Christ. She likes to use our family as one of her lecturing illustrations that very young children can and should be exposed to the gospel and led to Christ.

When she had explained all this to me, I was once more in awe of God and so very thankful that he would let our family be a small part of the wonderful work Mrs. Wisner and Childhood Evangelism are doing. Since that visit, Mrs. Wisner has been so thoughtful to send the children cards and treats on special occasions, and she even came out to our home one night and told them Bible stories. Truly the Lord has been so good to us.

And then came Shannon! With a burst of fireworks this little one exploded into our lives, bringing with him a full measure of love and joy. How I loved every inch of him, from the top of his little bald head right down to the tips of his tiny, pink toes.

He is blond and fair like Christa and me, with huge deep blue eyes and long curly eyelashes—but the general concensus is that he favors Mark more than the other children.

Like Mark and Christa, Shannon is bothered by allergies. I worried and worried over him during his first few weeks at home, because he had such a strange way of eating. He would seem hungry enough and would begin to take his bottle quite willingly; but after a few ounces he would start to fight it, twisting his little head back and forth and acting as if he were choking. Finally he would begin to cry and would refuse to drink any more milk at all. He wasn't gaining like I thought he should, and I was beginning to worry that he might be one of the failure-to-thrive babies I had heard of.

I was afraid to discuss this with the doctor. I'm not quite sure why. I suppose I thought he might tell me I was imagining things. Or worse yet, he might have an explanation for Shannon's behavior that I didn't want to hear.

However, when Shannon was six weeks old, Mike's brother Tucker and sister-in-law Nancy paid us a visit. Nancy, herself the mother of three girls, wanted to feed Shannon. She was horrified when he began his routine. "Donna," she told me firmly, "there is something wrong with this baby. You've just got to speak to the doctor about him."

Her comment was just the catalyst I needed to stir me into action. I phoned the pediatrician the very next day and was so relieved to be told that probably Shannon was allergic to milk. That seemed to be the very least of the different possibilities about which I had been worrying. Sure enough, a change in his formula to a soybean milk substitute immediately resolved the problem. Little Shannon began eating with gusto and gaining accordingly.

The other children are thrilled with their baby brother. Mark is ecstatic to have another boy in the family. "He's going to be great—just like me!" he says, and he can hardly wait to help him in sports.

Tara and Christa, who had actually hoped for a girl, have gotten over the fact that their baby is a boy. "Oh, I just love my baby brother so much," Tara often says. And Christa loves to play with him; she can get him to laugh at times when no one else can.

I can't imagine our family without this precious little boy. Whatever would we do without him? As always, God knew what was best for us.

It was a busy spring for the Nason family. Mark was thoroughly involved in his third year of Little League baseball and could hardly think of anything else. I loved to see my handsome son all dressed in his uniform and cap. And it makes me especially proud of Mike that with his busy schedule he has never missed one of Mark's games in all the years he has been playing organized sports. I know it means so much to Mark, and it has done a lot to build the wonderful relationship he and his dad share together.

Little Christa had her third birthday on April 10. Where did those three years go? She got to have her very first real birthday party and invited some of her little friends. Of course, big brother and sister were welcome, but Mark decided a room full of giggling three-year-old girls was a bit too much for him.

Shortly after Christa turned three, there was something special I wanted her to do. It was something I had always wanted to do and something I had dreamed of Tara doing: take dancing lessons! I found a dance studio that accepts three-year-olds and enrolled Christa in a combination ballet, tap, gymnastics, and modern dance class. How darling she looks in her black leotard and tights and tiny ballet slippers—just like a little doll. She loved dancing right from the start, and I hope it will help build in her a natural poise and grace of movement.

One Saturday morning bright and early, Tara and I set off on a great adventure—Blue Bird Mother-Daughter Camping Weekend. We drove out into the desert with her leader, Nancy Clark, and Nancy's two daughters Kelly and Danielle. It felt so strange to be going away for the weekend, leaving Mike to babysit Mark, Christa, and baby Shannon.

And yet of such are memories made. I know, because I have so many of them tucked away myself. My own dear mother was the fearless leader of my Brownie and Girl Scout troops from the time I was seven all the way up to age sixteen. I can remember countless camping trips she took with us. Days of sitting in damp tents in the drenching rain telling stories, nights of lying awake in the sweltering Texas heat, songs by the campfire, swimming in the creek.

When Tara had been born, these were the kinds of memories I had been determined to give her. I wanted to be her Scout leader as my mother had been mine. What a different life Tara and I have led than the one of which I had dreamed so long ago.

But here finally was our chance, and we were going to make the most of it. Rows of tents had already been set up when we arrived at Woodchuck Campgrounds. Thank goodness, one of the women's husbands came along to set up ours. After all those years of Girl Scouting, you would think I would have learned how to set up a tent!

All day long I tried to help Tara do all the things the other girls were doing. I pushed her up and down the hills on long hikes and took her to the water's edge to see the ducks swimming in the pond. I helped her with her craft project of making a figure out of pieces of wood and moss and berries we had found on our hike.

Tara had the fun of watching her dinner being cooked and eating it outdoors. But her favorite part of all, as it had always been mine, was the gathering together of all the girls around the campfire after dark and the singing of songs, both old and new. Tara knew most of them; and as I watched her pretty little face, glowing from the fire and intense in its singing, I was filled with such a longing. "Please, God," I cried, "there's got to be a way. Somehow, there's got to be a way."

After a rather uncomfortable night in our sleeping bags, we headed home, dirtier and wiser, and so much richer in memories.

It wasn't too many weeks later that Tara was able to share in yet another priceless camping experience. A year or so earlier, God had called a young physical therapist, Pat Hammon, into a wonderful and much-needed ministry among handicapped children and young adults.

His dream was so beautiful that I wondered why no one had thought of it before. Why not have a camp for handicapped children? A place where they could go for fun and recreation, a place where they could go to learn about God's great outdoors. Most of these young people were not as fortunate as Tara was to be included in a group such as Blue Birds. Before Pat founded Acampar, there was really nothing available for these children.

Pat also set up a program to reach these precious children's spiritual needs, which are every bit as important as their physical and social needs. He has Christian counselors to care for the children and to show them God's love. He has a program of Christian music and even Bible study for the older ones. He makes sure that no child leaves his camp without knowing that he is special, because God made him and loves him. All the children are taught that God has a special plan for their lives and that Jesus wants to live in their hearts. And who could possibly need to hear the message of God's love more than a handicapped child? I am so thankful to Pat for enabling my Tara, as well as all those like her here in Orange County, to have a part in something so special.

Tara loved her Acampar weekend and has never forgotten her wonderful counselor, Suzie Parks. If Suzie is an accurate example of the quality of people Pat has to work with the children, then he certainly has a winning team! Shortly after their return, we received the following letter from Suzie:

Dear Mr. and Mrs. Nason,

I wanted to share with you how much your Tara has meant to me and what an impact she has made on my life. Her sweet, loving spirit toward the Lord and people gives her an

inward beauty that shines to the world. She is so caring, and such determination I have never seen. She wanted to do everything herself, especially brush her hair. She has brought new strength to my ministry with these special people. One night at camp I was thinking of how frustrating it would be to not be able to use your hands for various things (like brushing your hair out of your face when you're trying to sleep). I decided right then and there that I wanted to give this little angel from God everything that I had to give. I just love her with all my heart. She has left me with a warmth I just can't explain. I can certainly see how God has used Tara to touch many lives.
May the Lord continually bless you,
Suzie Parks

The school year was drawing to a close, and we were anxious to evaluate Tara's progress. Her teacher, Maxine Nardulli, was elated with the advances Tara had made while in her class. Maxine, a tiny vivacious blonde, is exactly the kind of exuberant, loving person needed to work with orthopedically handicapped children. She is young and flexible, and willing to try practically anything to help the students in her care. She tailors individual learning programs for the children, to fit their own specific needs.

Due to Tara's extremely limited physical capacities, Maxine has really worked hard trying to come up with ideas and devices that will help make Tara as independent as possible and facilitate the learning process. By far the most exciting development in this area has been Tara's use of the typewriter. Maxine found a special headgear for Tara that has a long pointer on it. Tara's head control is good enough that she is able to aim the pointer where she wants it to go.

Tara's visual perception is so poor that when Maxine first mentioned trying her on the typewriter, I doubted that she would ever be able to read the letters on the keys. And I was right; she couldn't. But Maxine was undaunted. She was going to keep trying until she found a way. She finally hit upon the most unorthodox method of putting little clues next to certain letters. The M has a yellow dot on it, because the door to Mommy's bedroom is yellow; the V has a red heart to remind Tara of the V in love; there is a green arrow over the E and a red arrow over the T.

And it worked! As soon as these clues were attached, something clicked in Tara's brain and the entire keyboard fell into place. Maxine and some of the other teachers were in tears as they stood that day and watched Tara type her name. It was like a miracle, they said. I don't think it was just *like* a miracle; it *was* a miracle!

Since that fateful day, Tara has learned to type mommy, daddy, Mark, love, and I from memory. She could also type a few other simple words by copying them. If she could spell, we hoped she could eventually learn to read.

Tara had also learned to paint with watercolors, using her headgear, and was working on drawing with a pen held in her mouth like the famous quadriplegic artist Joni Eareckson, who has been a real inspiration to her. Tara has always loved to draw and color, but in previous attempts with her hands she has had to be content with scribbling. Now she could actually produce recognizable artwork, and she was so proud.

Tara had also made great progress with her swimming. She had learned to float on her back; and when she lost her floating "balance," she was learning to roll around to get onto her back again. She had learned to swim forward on her tummy, just slightly under the water, and to roll over onto her back when she ran out of air. Her instructor rolled her from the pool side into the water and was teaching her to immediately roll onto her back and float. Little by little, Tara was becoming pool-safe.

On July 2, Tara celebrated her eighth birthday. She had an outdoor party, and for the first time she had real friends to invite—friends she had made herself at school and through Blue Birds. It was wonderful to see all the girls playing happily together, and I was so proud of all of them.

In addition to her party, Tara was treated to another special birthday surprise. Garden Grove Community Church has so many dear members, one of whom is a woman by the name of Ginnie Gingras. Ginnie is a very talented seamstress, and her hobby is dressing dolls. Her home is full of all sorts of beautiful dolls—a real little girl's paradise!

She invited Tara over for her birthday, as she had the year before, and gave her a lovely Madame Alexander baby doll, complete with a wardrobe of clothes she had sewn and knitted herself. Tara loves dolls better than just about anything, and she was enthralled. It is a wondrous thing to see how very kind people can be.

Since R.H. Dana was holding three-hour summer school sessions each day, we decided to go ahead and send Tara. Our summer was already busy with Mark's and Tara's classes, but what would summer be without Forest Home? We spent a wonderful week there; eating and singing and studying the Bible and playing together as a family. And this summer there was an extra treat in store for us in the Christian Camping department. We had been invited to spend a week at Mount Hermon, another Christian camp located in Northern California in the Santa Cruz mountains. They asked us to bring our film about Tara and speak at one of their evening programs. That week was really special, and we enjoyed it so much. The only marring event was when five-month-old Shannon came down with bronchitis, but even that didn't dampen our spirits for long. The ten-hour drive back home in the car with a crying baby and three squealing children gave us quite a jolt, but Mike and I still felt the week had been well worth it.

After we returned home, we received several letters that were such a blessing to us. One of them, from the Macy family, was especially touching:

Dear Donna, Mike, and family,

We had such a marvelous week at Mt. Hermon this summer. However, this year was even more special and filled with "love pouring over" because of your precious Tara and your story and lives together.

We first heard of Tara from our little Jennifer who is six years old. She told us of her "new friend at Pioneer Camp who is in a wheelchair." Then on Tuesday night Jennifer was excited to tell us during the movie of Tara that "there she is—that's Tara!" She was moved to tears during the movie, as were we all. What a story of God's love, hope, and determination on all your parts.

Each day that week, Jennifer looked forward to sharing and being with Tara. We all fell "head over heels in love" with her. We were enchanted and captivated by her own sweet self—her especially delightful disposition. And in addition to that, she is so pretty. How could anyone resist?

Tara's story and yours is really an inspiration. And Tara has a real ministry of her own. How fortunate you are to be living lives that glorify God. I would love to do patterning for Tara. But since I can't do it for her, I plan to do it for some other little one near where we live. With great love, because of Tara, I am looking forward to starting.

You have all been in our prayers and on our minds since we have come home, and we wish you God's richest blessings!
With love and prayers,
The Macys
Jean, Dick, and Jennifer

All too soon our summer was over, and it was time to be getting the children ready to go back to school. What would the new school year hold for Mark and Tara? Success or defeat? Tara had a five-day evaluation at the Institutes coming up the last week in August. I don't think any of us were quite prepared for what was going to take place there.

CHAPTER ELEVEN
Tara's Trip

Mike and Tara flew into Philadelphia for the first time in nearly a year. The Institutes had sent a small group of people out to California in May, and Tara had been seen for a half-day evaluation at that time. Neither Art Sandler nor Glenn Doman had been a part of the May team, however, and Mike and I never really felt that Tara had been properly checked unless she had been seen by one of them.

We had gotten pretty good at predicting the kind of report Tara would get by noting the progress she was making at home. Although Tara was typing and swimming and her balance was better, we knew these were not the sorts of things Glenn would be looking for. We knew he would be pleased with her physical development, because she had grown two inches and gained ten pounds since her visit last year. However, we knew he would be very dissatisfied with Tara's neurological development. Her two problem areas, mobility and hand function, had remained virtually unchanged.

Even so, we weren't entirely prepared for the explosion which met Mike and Tara in Glenn's office. Glenn loves Tara and longs for her to get well. To sum up his feelings about Tara's progress in one word—he was *frustrated.* He had spent five years giving her the best program of neurological organization that he knew—programs that had worked miracles in the lives of some children. Why hadn't Tara improved the way he wanted her to?

He didn't know. And we didn't know. Certainly we had carried out Tara's prescribed programs to the best of our abilities. Certainly Tara had tried, although she had become discouraged over the past year. Only God knows why Tara's brain was not responding to the constant sensory stimulation we had been bombarding it with for five years. Could he have a different plan for her? One he hadn't yet revealed to us?

Once again we knew we had to trust God that he had a beautiful plan for Tara's life. And we had to remind ourselves once more that the most important thing for any person, including Tara, was not whether or not he or she could walk, but whether or not he was fulfilling the purpose for which he had been created; that purpose being to glorify God and enjoy him forever.

God's life plan is different and unique for

each individual. Some people may disagree with me, but I firmly believe that in God's providence he wills that some people can glorify and enjoy him better in a wheelchair than out of one. I don't like to admit it, but I must acknowledge that this is possibly the plan he has for Tara's life. I hope not, but I am willing to accept the fact that this may indeed be the case.

At any rate, we appeared to be at a crossroads. We had three immediate choices. We could continue with Tara the way we had the previous year, sending her to school half the day and patterning her half the day, and content ourselves with mediocre progress. Or we could cut out school altogether and begin to pattern Tara eight hours a day again. This, we felt, was unsatisfactory. Tara needed school, and we had no guarantee that her progress would improve if she stayed home. We could withdraw her from the Institutes' program altogether and look for help somewhere else. This we were unwilling to do at that particular time.

We had three alternatives, and we didn't like any of them. What were we going to do? It was Glenn who came up with the fourth choice. "If only Tara could come here to the Institutes for three or four months," he mused. "It's a shame I don't have a staff member with enough spare time to work with her. We need to get her crawling so well that we can start working on her creeping."

Mike thought immediately of Terry. "What if we could send Tara here with a friend who could administer her program under your supervision?"

"Do you know someone who could do it?" Glenn asked. "Someone who could spare the time from his own life? Someone Tara loves and respects and who will make her work?"

"I know the perfect person," Mike said enthusiastically. "Terry Patané! He's like a big brother to Tara, and she's very devoted to him. If anyone could get Tara to really apply herself and work hard, it would be Terry."

And so the dream was born. To send Tara and Terry to Philadelphia to live and to work for three months. But no, Mike and I both agreed, it seemed impossible. There were too many hurdles in the way. First of all, we didn't know if Terry would want to leave his job for three months. Of major concern was money. There was no way we could afford it! How could we even pay Terry and Tara's air fare back to Philadelphia? Much less rent them an apartment for three months, rent them a car, pay for their meals? No, it was out of the question. It would never work.

But if it was impossible, then why did it seem like such a good idea? We could use the three months as a testing ground to see if we should continue the patterning or look for other methods of therapy. If Tara couldn't improve in three months of intensive patterning done right at the Institutes, with an idea patterner like Terry administering her program, then what could we expect to accomplish at home?

Our insurance had never helped us pay for

Tara's visits to the Institutes, and that together with the plane fare to get there had wreaked havoc with our family finances long enough. For several months we had known that we couldn't continue taking Tara there on a permanent basis. But we wanted to give it one last try. For Tara to spend three months there seemed ideal.

"Let's just turn it over to the Lord," Mike said. "If he wants Tara and Terry to go, he will make a way for them. But he'll have to move fast. I want Tara home before Christmas, and I want her to spend three full months at the Institutes. That means that all the arrangements would have to be made so that they could leave for Philadelphia by September 15. That gives God two weeks. Let's see what he does."

If I had been present to watch God part the Red Sea and make a way for the Jews to escape from the Egyptians, I would have counted it no greater miracle than to see him make the way for Tara and Terry to go to Philadelphia. So beautifully did the Lord provide for this trip, that every minute detail was taken care of. Within two weeks it was all accomplished, and it left us breathless to watch the speed with which God worked.

The first miracle was Terry himself—the very fact that we had this fine young man for a friend and that he cared so much about Tara. He had helped with her so many times, and he knew exactly how to take care of her. He had devoted a large part of the past two years to working with Tara and knew her routine inside and out. He possessed just the right mixture of discipline and love to persuade her to work her hardest. And he was pleased to give up three months of his life to help Tara in Philadelphia. How many twenty-three-year-old men would leave their jobs and travel across the country to play mother and father to a helpless eight-year-old girl and accept no money in return?

The second miracle was the air fare. Merrill Eichenberger, who worked at the church, had become friends with Rudy Markmiller, the owner of a company called Network Courier Service. The business of this organization was to transport videotapes and other materials for the television networks from Los Angeles to New York and vice versa. They accomplished this by sending an employee on the all-night flight from Los Angeles to New York each evening. They would put all the materials in the baggage compartment, and he would carry all the baggage stubs and give them to another employee who met the plane in New York.

We were told that if Terry would be the courier and carry the baggage stubs, Network Courier would pay for his airline ticket. That way we only had to pay for Tara's fare. "Thank you, Lord!" we shouted.

We now had a way to get Terry and Tara to Philadelphia. But what could we do with them after they arrived? We needed a place for them to live which would be near the Institutes, preferably for free. How could we ever find an apartment rent-free? And if we could, how would Terry and Tara eat? Terry couldn't cook, and we couldn't afford to have them eat out in restaurants.

Our dear friend, Pastor Charles Murray of the Oreland Presbyterian Church, had a wonderful idea. Within a ten-mile radius of both the church and the Institutes was the international headquarters of Worldwide Evangelization Crusade. It housed the business end of the group and was also a training ground for missionaries, as well as a place for them to live when they are home on sabbatical.

The director of WEC is Sam Werdal, and he and his wife, Esther, had been attending Chuck's church. Pastor Murray spoke to the Werdals, asking if there might not be a vacant room at WEC where Terry and Tara might stay. He explained to them about the book and movie about Tara, and said she was kind of a missionary herself.

The Werdals conferred with the other missionaries there at WEC. In order for Terry and Tara to live there, it would have to be the unanimous decision of the group. Frankly, they weren't sure. What kind of unforeseen problems could arise with a little crippled girl living in their midst? But in the end their compassion won out. Terry and Tara could live at WEC rent-free. WEC has a large dining room in which the women take turns preparing and serving meals to the group. Terry and Tara could eat with them; all they asked was that Terry drop whatever money they could afford each week into the box in the kitchen. All the missionaries who live there are asked to do the same to help cover the cost of the meals.

This arrangement was so beautiful, I could hardly believe it was true. How wonderful that God had placed Terry and Tara in a community of Christians who would love them and pray for them and look out for them. It was a family situation, and there would be children there for Tara to play with. It was perfect!

That still left us with the problem of transportation. With Tara in her wheelchair, taking the bus was impossible. We couldn't afford to rent a car, and yet Terry and Tara needed some way to get from WEC to the Institutes each day.

Chuck Murray decided to see what he could do. He just walked off the street one day into the largest car dealership in the area, Bryner Chevrolet, and asked to see the sales director. He explained to him all about Tara and about how she and Terry needed a car. "Oh, I couldn't help you there," the sales director replied. "You'd have to speak with the owner." We were surprised that he didn't give him a flat "no," but went to the trouble of referring him to his superior.

A few days later Chuck had an appointment with Chuck Peterson, the owner of Bryner Chevrolet. He took a copy of our book *Tara* with him, so Mr. Peterson would understand the situation. He took one look at the book and said, "I know that little girl. I've seen her on Hour of Power." And that is how we were given a car for Terry to drive. Oreland Presbyterian Church was even kind enough to attach a rider onto their insurance policy so that the car would be covered in case of accident.

It was a miracle—all those seemingly impossible details worked out in less than two weeks! How powerful God is and how loving.

"There was a time when I could be skeptical about God," Terry said, "but not anymore. I've seen him work miracles, and I know he cares for me."

Now I was on the spot! In a matter of a few days I had to finish getting Mark and Christa ready to start school and completely pack Tara up for a three-month trip. There were so many last-minute details to attend to. Tara needed warm nightgowns and bodysuits and sweaters. I also decided to take the plunge and get Tara's hair cut. Her new short style is so cute and makes her look so grown up.

When I called R.H. Dana School, Tara's teacher, Maxine, was especially disappointed that Tara would be missing the first three months of school. I felt badly too; it was just another case of it being impossible to fit everything of benefit into the life of a child like Tara. It was also another illustration of the old adage—you can't please everyone.

I think the parents of children with problems probably feel the pressure of trying to keep everyone happy more than most people do. Everybody wants to help, everyone has advice to offer, and none of it is the same. I've often had people ask me what the prognosis is for Tara's future. About all I can tell them is, "Who knows? Take her to ten different doctors and you'll get ten different answers and ten different reasons why." The professionals (as well as the well-meaning friends and relatives) whose suggestions we follow think we're terrific, and the ones we don't agree with think we're crazy and insensitive.

What are we to do? We're Tara's parents, and

we love her more than anyone else does. We're the ones who are ultimately responsible for her care. We listen to everyone, discuss all the pros and cons, pray about it, and in the end must make the decisions on our own. Sometimes we make the right decisions, sometimes we don't. We just have to content ourselves with the knowledge that we always do the best we can.

I think Dr. Spock sums it up so well in his book *How to Care for Your Disabled Child* when he says: "Grandparents, other relatives, and family friends who are concerned for the welfare of the handicapped child may still have no real understanding of his disability or his treatment. They can be quite a trial to the parents, with their persistent errors and suggestions." Mike and I try to temper our reaction to this problem with love, realizing that it is love for Tara that prompts all the advice. I guess that is why we often feel sad that we can't please everybody, because each loves so much.

At any rate, the evening of Saturday, September 11 came way too soon. We took Tara out to dinner and came home and presented her with an ice cream cake. We sang "Happy Trip to You" to the tune of "Happy Birthday." Then we all gathered on the couch for prayer. Mike led us in a beautiful prayer, asking the Lord to watch over Tara and Terry and get them safely to Philadelphia. We asked him to bless their trip and to make it a special time of growth for both of them. We asked him to help them not to be lonely. At the end of the prayer, Tara burst into tears. Mike's eyes were moist and so were mine. Christa looked at us, and she began to cry. Even Mark was unusually quiet. Only six-month-old Shannon seemed unperturbed.

We were able to quiet the girls down and tuck Christa into bed before it was time to drive to the airport. During the summer Terry's family had moved sixty miles away to Upland, California; so they would be meeting us at the terminal.

His parents and his sister Tina all looked so serious. Terry, who had actually never been away from home before for more than a few days, was really nervous. I had a feeling that the adjustment would be much harder for him than it would be for Tara. And I had a premonition that the trip itself would do more for Terry than it would for Tara. Shy and insecure, he would be forced into new situations which would help him grow. He was leaving Los Angeles a boy, but I had a feeling he would be a man when he returned. I think his folks, with that peculiar mixture of hope and dread common to parents, sensed this too.

It was hard to say good-bye; even though we knew they were on the brink of a great adventure, we knew how much we would miss them. The Patanés and Mike and I stood at the terminal window a long time, staring into the dark night sky. Then they were gone.

What would my life be like without Tara? I couldn't imagine, but I was anxious to find out. I could go on a diet, join a Bible study, write, play more with the other children, visit my neighbors. I realized that after six years of almost nonstop caring for Tara, I was going to have a rest. And I was going to enjoy it!

But the next morning the house didn't seem

quite the same. Mike and Mark had left at 5:30 a.m. as they always do on Sundays to begin working on the production of Hour of Power. I was left alone with Christa and Shannon. There was no little voice calling, "Mommy, I need to go potty. Mommy, my leg hurts. Mommy, I want to sit up in bed." And there was no Terry laughing and teasing as he helped me bathe and dress the children for church. My daughter and one of my best friends were gone, and it would be a long time before I would see them again.

Terry and Tara had flown all night across the country and landed in the early morning hours in New York City. Terry had found the Network Courier man without too much trouble and had given him all the baggage stubs. Then they had boarded another plane and taken the thirty-five-minute flight into Philadelphia. Ruth Seals met them at the plane and drove them to her home in Oreland, where they would stay for the first two days.

They were both exhausted and slept a good part of the day. When he awoke, Terry was greeted by the sights and sounds and smells of a totally new and different part of the country. California born and raised, he had never been to the East before and it was a unique experience for him. He immediately loved the quaint architecture and the big trees of Pennsylvania.

For Tara, the lush green Pennsylvania countryside was almost as familiar as the rolling sagebrush-covered hills of Mission Viejo. She was in a home she knew, with people she loved, and she was trying to figure out how long three months actually was and what exactly it meant to be away from home for that length of time.

Terry, on the other hand, knew exactly how long three months was, and was also pretty sure he didn't want to be gone from home for that long. He felt the heavy burden of being solely responsible for Tara, and hoped he had made the right decision in coming. Still, he was there, and he had promised the Nasons, and he wasn't going to let them down, no matter what!

On Monday, Terry and Tara concentrated on adjusting to the three-hour time difference between Los Angeles and Philadelphia. They also went to Bryner Chevrolet to pick up the car. Terry had been so worried that it would have manual transmission, which he didn't know how to drive. But I knew the Lord would take better care of them than that! As it turned out, it was a very nice copper-colored 1976 Chevrolet Malibu Classic with automatic transmission, and Terry was delighted.

The next day the Seals family watched Tara, and Terry drove to WEC to meet the Werdals and see the room where he and Tara would be living. "I bet it will be some old algae-covered monastery with water leaking down the walls and depressing-looking people walking around," Terry had jokingly forecasted before they left California. He's definitely not a possibility thinker!

I wasn't really worried about what he would find at WEC, but I was surprisingly relieved when he called excitedly to tell me how happy he was with his and Tara's new home.

"Donna," Terry bubbled over the phone, "we

have our own little apartment. It's even got a kitchen in it with a refrigerator and a stove and everything! They said they have an extra television set and will be setting it up in our room tonight."

"Oh, Terry," I said in a voice overcome with emotion. "Praise the Lord!" It was so much more than we had dared to dream of! I had anticipated a small, sparsely furnished room; nothing more. I figured they would probably have to share a bath. The idea of a kitchen and a television set had never even occurred to me. An actual little apartment—it was too wonderful!

Lois Steele, who was in charge of guest accommodations at WEC, had led Terry into the main building (which was actually an old Philadelphia mansion) and started up the first of several flights of stairs en route to his and Tara's room. Terry had tried to disguise his dismay, but something about his expression caused Lois to stop and ask, "Are stairs OK for you?"

"Well, they're all right," Terry had stammered, "but Tara *is* in a wheelchair."

"A wheelchair! Of course; I should have realized. All these stairs will never do, but I have just the place for you. Follow me."

She led Terry out of the building and over to a modern two-story structure which houses many of the families there. "This apartment was built especially for a woman in a wheelchair," Lois explained, indicating a door on the first floor. "It has ramps and everything."

Terry and Tara moved their belongings into

their apartment at WEC that very afternoon, and that evening they ate their first meal in the big dining room. Terry was immediately impressed with the atmosphere of love that pervaded the room. The families were gathered around the large tables, and Esther explained to Terry that he and Tara would be sitting with a different family each week so that they would get acquainted.

Several of the children came over to greet Tara and tell her they were glad she had come. One little eight-year-old blonde introduced herself as Laurie Longenecker. "We've been praying for a girl my age for me to have for a friend," she confided, "and here you are."

The wonderful people at WEC accepted Terry and Tara into their fellowship and showed them the greatest of love and concern. The women even offered to help Terry with their laundry. Esther Werdal wrote me the loveliest letter to let me know that they were all looking out for Terry and Tara, and that they were upholding both them and our families at home in prayer. Once again I just praised God that he had arranged for Terry and Tara to stay in such a perfect place. He is so good and so able to take care of all our needs!

The next day was to be a very exciting one for Terry. Since he had first met our family two years earlier, one of his greatest desires had been to visit the Institutes. And here was a dream come true. He was able to spend two days in new parent seminars there, listening to lectures explaining the Institutes' treatment methods.

Tara spent the two days with the group of

first-time children while their parents were attending the seminars with Terry. Art Sandler, who hadn't seen Tara since her visit the year before, did not know she was there. He spotted her across the room full of children, assuming that she also was a new patient, and called over another staff member. "That little girl looks just like Tara Nason," he said, "except that she's older and has short hair."

He walked over and studied her closely, amazed that two children could look so much alike. He called yet another staff member over, and the two of them discussed the resemblance. Meanwhile, Tara sat there quietly and didn't open her mouth. Many of the children who come to the Institutes are unable to speak, and Art assumed that this little girl was similarly afflicted.

Finally he called Gretchen Kerr, the one staff member who was aware of Tara's presence. "Look at this!" he exclaimed. "Doesn't this little girl look like Tara Nason?"

Gretchen was surprised. "That is Tara Nason!"

At this point, Tara burst into peals of mischievous laughter, enjoying the joke she had played on her friends.

That Monday Tara and Terry began the work that had brought them to Philadelphia. They were shown to a small room upstairs in the old mansion that houses part of the Institutes' facilities. Tara's program was a simple one; crawling, crawling, and more crawling.

The first week she was to crawl ten feet in

two minutes. Terry had her crawl the ten-foot-long room over and over again and timed her each time. In between her crawls, Terry worked with her on a series of small flashcards. Each one had a different picture on it. There were birds and animals as well as historic and geographic locations.

He showed her the picture and told her what it was, then went on to the next card. That first week they started with sixty pictures which the Institutes called Bits, short for Bits of Information.

In addition to this, Tara wore her mask for sixty seconds out of every five minutes just as she does at home. This breathing into a plastic bag, which automatically stimulates deep, even breathing, is one of the major reasons why Tara has such strong, disease-resistant lungs.

That first week Tara began crawling the ten feet in two-and-one-half to three minutes. She was wildly inconsistent, which is normal for her, but once during the week she did break her goal. She crawled the ten feet in one minute, fifty-eight seconds. That was to be the only time in the entire three months that she was able to reach her goal.

There was one part of Tara's program that was missing, the actual crawling patterns themselves. With Tara's continued growth, she now required five people to properly administer her patterns; one at the head and one at each arm and leg.

Unfortunately, there was not the group of international children living and working at the Institutes that there had been during Tara's and my Christmas stay. Gretchen arranged for students from the college for neurologically handicapped young people, which is housed there on the Institutes' grounds, to help Terry with Tara's patterns. But the young men and women just didn't have the gross motor coordination so necessary to put Tara's stiff limbs through the crawling motions. Obviously, other arrangements would have to be made. But what?

Terry decided to seek help from Oreland Presbyterian Church. Pastor Murray announced Tara's need for patterners from the pulpit that Sunday, and it was wonderful to see how the women responded. In no time, Terry had a patterning team of some twenty-five local women who were anxious to help. Each one promised an hour of her time each week, just as our patterners do at home. Esther Werdal was kind enough to accept the difficult job of coordinator for the week, making sure that the pattern hour each day was staffed with enough women.

Rather than have twenty-five women traipsing in and out of the Institutes each week, it seemed better to do the patterns at WEC. In the basement of Terry and Tara's building, Terry discovered a large unfurnished room carpeted with indoor-outdoor carpet. It was a natural for patterning. Had he and Tara been living anywhere else, I'm sure such a room would not have been available to them.

In addition to a large carpeted room, another necessity for patterning is the pattern table itself. When families go on the Institutes' program, they usually have to have a table custom-built for this purpose. It must be the proper height for people to stand and work at, so as not to injure their backs. It must be just the right width to allow the child to lie comfortably, with enough room for his arms and legs to be moved up and down. The table must also be padded and covered with vinyl.

This table could have been a real stumbling block to Tara's patterns at WEC, but God provides. Terry found a table built almost exactly to the Institutes' specifications downstairs in the basement. The women had been using it as a table on which to sort and fold laundry.

Isn't it wonderful to know that the God who runs the universe is also interested in the little everyday things that are important to us? Before we even knew that Terry and Tara would be coming to Philadelphia, God had the room and the pattern table ready and waiting for them.

The working situation at WEC was so ideal that eventually Terry began to do all of Tara's program there, going into the Institutes periodically for evaluation and new suggestions.

And the women were so kind to Tara, bringing her little treats to brighten her days. Helen Kuleskey, one of the missionaries at WEC, began a beautiful book of leaves for her. Each week when she came, she brought new and different leaves from the many beautiful trees which are in such abundance there.

Terry and Tara were settling in, beginning to feel at home in their new surroundings, starting to make special new friends. Terry wrote to me every day, keeping me posted on all their activities and sending me detailed reports of Tara's progress. I wrote to Tara and Terry each day also, and tried to send Tara a little love gift each week. About every other week, I mailed them a large batch of homemade fudge. Many of Tara's friends and patterners here in Mission Viejo also found time to mail her cards and letters and treats.

Tara had been extremely homesick for the first week or so, but being a gregarious child she soon bounced back and entered into her new life with gusto. She had one thing at WEC that she didn't have at home, a very best friend her own age.

She and Laurie Longenecker spent hours together playing dolls. They gave them baths and shampoos and just had a wonderful time. One night Tara was crawling on the floor, and Laurie was having fun playing with her wheelchair. She was sitting in it and racing it around the house. Tara looked up at her friend and said, "You like it? I'll sell it to you for fifty bucks!" Then she and Laurie both dissolved into giggles.

Terry had also been very lonely the first few weeks and had fought valiantly against depression. But gradually, almost reading between the lines, I began to notice a different tone to his letters. There was something happening to him, something special. He was facing difficult situations, and he was meeting them head-on and conquering them. He was gaining enormous self-respect and was making many new friends.

Things were working out nicely on the homefront as well. Mark had settled into his school routine and was working hard. Little Christa was becoming more grown-up every day. She is, I am sure, the prissiest little girl in the whole world. She seemed to have been born with the knowledge of how to toss her blonde curls saucily and bat her eyelashes over her enormous blue eyes, while at the same time opening them up even wider. "Well, Mommy," she told me in that haughty little voice of hers, one hand on her hip and the other held outstretched, "you know I'm just a little girl, and I miss my big sister."

One day a tape arrived from Philadelphia. Terry and Tara had recorded different parts of their day on it for us. Christa sat enraptured for an entire hour listening to her sister's voice, her little face pressed nose to nose with the tape recorder as if trying to get as close to Tara as possible. And yet whenever she had a chance to talk to Tara on the telephone, Christa would only explode into laughter and say "Silly billy has a berry," which was her favorite phrase at the time.

I had worried that the three-month separation might in some way erode the beautiful friendship between my two daughters. But it didn't; the bonds of love were too strong.

Back in Philadelphia, Terry and Tara were working hard, but they were also having fun. There were wheelchair runs through the crispy autumn leaves and Monday night's viewing of *Little House on the Prairie* with the three Steele children, whose parents were missionaries staying at WEC. They were often invited out to dinner in the homes of friends and members of the church.

One day in early October, Terry told me in one of our frequent phone conversations, "I think Tara and I will drive down to Washington, D.C., this weekend before the weather gets bad." Washington is only a five-hour drive from Philadelphia, and Terry had never been there. Tara had visited our nation's capital only once at the age of three, and this seemed like a perfect opportunity for both learning and fun.

That weekend turned out to host the worst rainstorm of the year. High winds and heavy rains battered a large area of the East Coast, bringing with them tornadoes in several states. But Terry had planned a trip to Washington, and he wasn't going to let rain interfere.

He and Tara drove through the pelting rain, enjoying the sound it made as it pounded the roof of the car. Fortunately, it cleared in Washington late that afternoon so that they were able to see the sights. Tara had been learning the different monuments and historic places in Washington on her Bit cards, and it was fun for her to see them all in person. She sometimes has trouble transferring visual knowledge, so we were especially pleased that she was able to recognize the historic sites from the pictures on the cards.

All that month I looked forward to one thing; my four-day visit to Philadelphia scheduled for Halloween weekend. It was the midpoint in Tara's three-month absence, and my excitement was really mounting. I was going to act as courier of the videotapes, as Terry had done, to help pay for my airfare. So I left on the 11:00 plane from Los Angeles and flew all night, arriving in New York in the early morning hours.

I transferred to a small local airplane for the short trip into Philadelphia and had planned to sleep all the way there. But once we were up in the air, I became completely mesmerized by the beauty of the fall landscape beneath me. We were flying quite low, and in the early morning light the air was crisp and clean. Below me lay the patchwork of autumn. Golds, oranges, reds, russets, and browns stretched as far as the eye could see. The woods were everywhere, and it seemed to me that each leaf had been delicately tinted and blended by the unseen hand of the Master Artist.

"O Lord," I whispered, "this California girl sure does love the East." When I think of such beauty conceived and carried out in the mind of God, it makes me ever more aware of the genius of the Creator. I can only stand before him in awestruck praise.

As we landed in Philadelphia, my soaring spirits virtually exploded in a burst of emotion. I felt like running from the plane and throwing my arms around Tara and never letting go. But being a rather subdued person, I walked with as much composure as I could muster through the terminal until I caught sight of the familiar blue wheelchair with its dark-haired, bright-eyed occupant. I saw the tall, moustached figure beside her.

"Mommy!" Tara let out a yell, kicking her

legs and bouncing up and down in her chair excitedly. "Oh, Tara," I said as I buried my face in her thick brown hair. "And Terry," as I grasped his outstretched hand.

What a wonderful weekend we spent together! The autumn air was cool and crisp, such a welcome change from the ninety-degree heat I had left in Los Angeles. But the best part was seeing for myself that all was well with Tara and Terry. Their bright smiles told me that!

As we rounded the corner and started up the hill that is the home of Worldwide Evangelization Crusade, I was struck once more by the beauty of the setting. The hill was heavily wooded, and the trees were a veritable explosion of color. At the top stood the majestic old gray-stone mansion house, to its left the green two-story apartment building where Terry and Tara lived. Yet a third structure, made of gray stone with an old-fashioned clock tower, graced the lovely grounds.

When I had shown my neighbor, Francie Thomas, photographs of WEC that Terry had sent me, she had said it looked like it came right out of a fairy tale. And she was right; it did. The grass was covered with brightly colored leaves, and I did my best to shuffle through each one of them, delighting in the cacophony of crackles and crunches they made beneath my feet.

Terry and Tara settled me down for a much-needed rest while they drove in for an evaluation appointment at the Institutes. After their session, Terry put a clear plastic briefcase full of all Tara's medical records on top of the car while he lifted her inside and folded up and stored her wheelchair. Stuffed into the briefcase were five years' worth of irreplaceable Institutes' records as well as the charts and graphs Terry had been keeping on Tara during their stay. Terry was solely responsible for them, but somehow he forgot to take them off the roof before they started back to WEC. In fact, he forgot about them entirely and didn't even realize they were missing when he got Tara back out of the car and headed for the basement to work more on her program.

That evening Ruth Hutchby, one of Tara's Philadelphia patterners, called on the phone to ask if Terry was missing some of Tara's records. At that instant, his heart sank, as he remembered that he had left the valuable papers on the roof. I had to blink back tears when I realized how carefully God had been protecting those records.

The plastic briefcase had blown off the car top on Stenton Avenue, which is a very heavily trafficked thoroughfare. Of all the people who no doubt noticed the reams of paper blowing through the air, one man in particular decided to stop his car on this busy street and investigate. Ray Edwards has never before or since stopped his car for something in the street, but this time he did. The plastic briefcase was gone, as were Terry's charts and graphs, of which I had copies at home, but every single one of the Institutes' irreplaceable records was there! Not only that, but this man recognized Tara's name and knew she was somehow connected with Oreland Presbyterian Church.

He was able to get in touch with Ruth, who returned the records to us.

Even though I know God is omnipotent, I never cease to be amazed when I see such an overt example of his power. And it is not just his power I see here, but his love, his willingness to get involved with human beings on a day-to-day basis. How kind it was of him to spare Terry and me the worry of knowing that the records were missing. We didn't realize it until they had been found, and I shudder to think of how upsetting our day would have been had we known earlier. It is so wonderful for me to have Jesus for my best friend. He's always there when I need him, and he never lets me down.

It was with very grateful hearts that we prepared for our evening meal that night. Tara was so excited, because this was WEC's semiannual Fun Night. Since it was only two days until Halloween, the children were to wear their costumes to dinner.

Tara was going to be a Japanese lady. When our book *Tara* was being translated into Japanese, Mrs. Kiyoko Ishii, who did the actual translating, paid us a visit. She lived in Tokyo and was a fascinating house guest. Shortly after her return to Japan, she sent Tara a lovely Japanese kimono, and it was in this that I dressed her for the Fun Night.

Tara and I had such a good time as I put mascara on her eyelashes and powdered her face white. When we were through, she looked like a beautiful Japanese lady, and she was so thrilled.

After dinner all the children who lived there on the hill went trick-or-treating among the various living quarters there. What fun Terry and I had pushing Tara up and down the hills through the fallen leaves in the frosty night air. The group of costumed children of all ages was scampering about, laughing and talking. They were so kind and so friendly to Tara, treating her just like one of the gang, and again I was so thankful to God for bringing her to WEC.

Later that night all the missionaries and staff of WEC and neighboring Christian Literature Crusade gathered for a time of fun and fellowship. It was a costume party, the first I had been to since my childhood. Terry and I went as Jack and Jill, complete with bucket, although we were usually mistaken for Tom Sawyer and Alice in Wonderland.

In the meeting room of the old mansion, some fifty of us gathered. There were children as small as my baby Shannon all the way up to senior citizens, all in costume. They had obviously spent considerable time in preparation for their skits, and nearly everyone had a part to play. They poked good-natured fun at just about everyone, and I laughed until the tears came streaming down my cheeks.

Where else in this jaded, complicated world, except in a group of dedicated Christians like these, could you find so many people having so much fun with no outside help? There was no liquor, no drugs, no cigarettes, no vulgarity; just a bunch of God's people having a wonderful time.

"Lord," I thought, "I think Christians must

be the happiest people on earth, for you can teach us how to have fun simply."

I don't think I will ever forget that night spent with the missionaries at WEC. I will never forget the feeling of God's love and acceptance that was present there. And I really appreciated for the first time the unique position Terry and Tara were in to be able to share for a while in the lives of these remarkable people.

The following day we took Tara into Lancaster County to see the beautiful farms and picturesque homes of the Pennsylvania Dutch. Then we drove to Hershey and took a tour of the chocolate factory. I was so glad she could have these learning experiences. Even though she was missing three months of school, she was being exposed to a lot of knowledge on an experiential level, and this I felt was very good.

Sunday found us attending services at Oreland Presbyterian Church. Pastor Murray was speaking on the subject "I Am Special," and I was so thrilled when he used Tara and Terry as one of his illustrations.

"One of the most beautiful things that happened to me last week," he began, "was when I had the privilege of going to Worldwide Evangelization Crusade to see a group of women working with Terry Patané in patterning Tara. It's hard work; and it's a beautiful thing that they're doing. They're being used by God as somebody very special to work in Tara's life to help her with healing.

"I can't tell you the admiration that I have

for Terry. And it was a privilege to gather with him afterward and to just talk for a little bit, Tara resting in his arms. The others had left, and Terry said to me, 'You know, people pray for Tara—they're praying all over the United States. Some people are asking the questions, Why isn't she healed? Why doesn't she get better immediately? With all those prayers? With all that faith? Why?'

"Terry and I talked about it, and we decided that the real miracle is God's touch of life and not so much whether a healing occurs instantaneously or slowly. God is at work in his way and for his purposes.

"And then Terry went on to say, 'You know, if it hadn't been for Tara's handicap I might never have known Jesus. I might never have known the Lord. I might never have come to know her parents and to find Christ through Donna.'

"Boy, I'll tell you—Tara is somebody special. And you—you are somebody special too!"

It meant so much to me to hear these words; to know that Tara's life was being used to glorify God; to realize that she and Terry had a special job to do —even in Philadelphia, so far from home.

The next day was Monday, my last day. I would be flying home on the 11:00 plane from New York that night; and while I missed my family, I also hated to have to leave Tara and Terry behind. Sometimes emotions can get so confused; I'm glad I don't have to rely on them altogether in decision-making matters.

That morning one of Tara's patterners, Ruth

Bessey, had a lovely coffee for me. She had invited Tara's entire patterning team, as well as many of the women from WEC. It was so touching for me to meet all the kind souls who were helping Tara there. As first one and then another told of the blessing Tara had been to them personally, I just praised God again for using my daughter in this very special ministry.

All too soon the day was over, and darkness crept across the sky and covered the land. It was time for me to leave. I hugged Tara so tightly there in the terminal. How could I stand to leave her? As I looked out the window from the plane, I could see Tara and Terry gazing out through the airport glass. I knew they couldn't see me, but I waved and waved, hoping that somehow they would feel my love and sense my great reluctance in leaving.

Somehow I managed to get myself and my luggage from one terminal to another at John F. Kennedy Airport in New York City, and aboard the big jumbo jet. Oh, how I hated to fly all night alone! Before me lay the great expanse of black night sky—and home.

Back in Mission Viejo, I slipped easily into my normal routine. Chauffeuring Mark back and forth from private to public school three mornings a week; picking up Christa from preschool; driving her to music and dancing lessons; going to Bible study; helping Mark with his homework and his paper route; and now there was Christmas shopping to do. The weeks sped by, each one busier than the one before.

Mike and I were using some of our time to work with Steve Koska, who was trying to establish a special kind of home for brain-injured children. Himself an ordained minister and the father of an aphasic daughter named Bethany, Steve had the vision of a Christian interim care facility for children brain-injured after birth.

Not a day goes by but that someone's perfect child crosses over the border from normalcy into the hazy world of brain injury. A strong, healthy boy careens down a street on his skateboard and crashes into a parked car, a baby falls down the stairs, a little girl is accidentally hit in the head playing baseball. And in an instant, their entire lives and those of their families are changed forever.

These children are rushed to hospitals in siren-blaring ambulances and worked over night and day in intensive-care wards. They are medicated and monitored and operated on; and when their lives are out of danger, no one knows what to do with them. They are no longer "sick" in the classic sense, and do not belong in the hospital.

But they are certainly far from well, and the constant special care they require can hardly be provided at home. So what is done with these broken little minds and bodies? They are shunted off to state mental hospitals or to geriatric convalescent homes.

When this happens, what becomes of the child? How can he or she ever hope to fight his way back to normalcy in such abnormal surroundings? How can a recently brain-injured child, who needs to be constantly bombarded with stimulation, possibly be stimulated while wasting away in a bed surrounded by profoundly retarded individuals or elderly sick people?

These are the problems Steve Koska and his wife, Charla, want to solve here in Orange County, which is the fastest growing county in the country. And Mike and I were so happy that they asked us to help them by joining their board of directors.

Bethany Manor will be a live-in, Christ-centered home where children can go between the hospital and their own individual homes. It will provide loving care, tailored especially to the very unique needs of the recently brain-injured. It will also make use of constant intense therapy which is so necessary if these children are to ever take their rightful places in the world.

But more than that, it will give spiritual help to the families of these children. I've been there, and I know the intense sense of loss and mourning these parents go through. They need a very special kind of counseling, and Bethany Manor hopes to provide it; hopes to help pick up the broken pieces of shattered dreams and show how they can begin to fit back together again.

And then, as the child improves and is able to go home on a permanent basis and begin to rebuild his life, Bethany Manor hopes to have an out-patient clinic where he can return for evaluation and therapy.

It's a big dream, and big dreams are

expensive in both time and money. In early December, the board decided to hold its first fund-raising dinner. I prayed that the Lord would show me just whom to invite to this affair, and the other board members did the same. The result was an excellent turnout and a very special evening.

Mike and I were so thankful to be able to show the movie *Tara* that night as part of the program, for it so clearly illustrates the need for a place such as Bethany Manor. We were also able to donate *Tara* books, so that each family present would have a better understanding of the world of brain injury and the impact it has on the life of the family.

Steve closed the evening by reading an amplification of the words of Jesus taken from Matthew 25, which Steve wrote with the brain-injured in mind. It so touched my heart that I wanted to share it here.

" 'I WAS HUNGRY AND YOU GAVE ME FOOD TO EAT.' I was starved for love and you loved me. I was hungry for companionship and you spent time with me. I needed someone to hold me and you held me so tightly, so close to you; you stroked my cheek and my brow and you kissed me. I was hungry, spiritually; just like any other human being I had a void in me that only Jesus could fill. And you shared Jesus Christ with me; you read the Bible to me, told me about Jesus, and prayed with me.

" 'I WAS THIRSTY AND YOU GAVE ME WATER.' My mind was going stale from inactivity. When others assumed that my injury and handicap also meant that I was now dumb and stupid, they began to treat me that way. They talked down to me. And it wasn't too long until they didn't talk to me at all. But every time you were with me, you conversed with me. You made me feel that you wanted to hear from me; that I had something valuable and of interest to share with you. It refreshed me; it stimulated me; you kept my mind fertile and alert. You would not let me regress and slip into nothingness.

" 'I WAS A STRANGER AND YOU INVITED ME IN.' I had a brain injury and suddenly I was very different. I certainly didn't ask for this to happen, but it did. I was different; I acted differently; my behavior was unusual and abnormal. I did things that were strange to you, but you still loved me. You still wanted me around. I even hurt you, caused you to be embarrassed, but that didn't make any difference. Even when my needs caused you some real problems and required you to radically change your life-style, you still loved me and you made sure that I knew it. I couldn't respond to you properly; yet you invited me into your family, your home, your life, and your world.

" 'I WAS NAKED AND YOU CLOTHED ME.' I had no defense; nothing to cover or shield me from the cruel stares and cold ridicule of insensitive, uncaring, and vicious people. Even though I couldn't adequately respond or protect myself, I understood everything they said and I cried inside. You knew it and you came, bundled me up in the warmth of your love, and made sure that I was at peace.

" 'I WAS SICK AND YOU VISITED ME.' You didn't forget me; you didn't consider my situation as hopeless; you didn't give up on me. You encouraged me. You lovingly prodded me on; you worked with me, taught me, and ministered the love and power of God to me.

"You kept coming back again and again. You imparted your strength and hope to me. As you gave your time and your love to me, you were actually giving yourself to me.

" 'I WAS IN PRISON AND YOU CAME TO ME.' I was trapped and confined, sentenced for life in the very real prison of my injured brain and unresponsive, unresponding body. You gave your time, talent, wealth, and love to provide for me the environment, treatment, equipment, and personnel who could help me, and slowly, but ever so surely, you released me."

This sentiment so beautifully sums up my feelings for all of Tara's patterners and all of the other people who have shown her such love, both here and in Philadelphia. It is so wonderful to look around and see that God's people are still showing their love for Christ by helping those in need!

Across the country in Philadelphia, Tara and Terry were winding up their three-month stay. It had been eventful in so many ways, both for us and for them. It had given Mike and me a chance to really think clearly about Tara and about her future. Freed from the constant physical care, we seemed to be able to consider the various alternatives more objectively, and this was good.

One of the things I came to realize was the fact that I would need to more carefully budget my time among the four children when Tara returned. Tara would need me, but so would the others. I determined to see if I could arrange for the patterners to take over more of her program, so that I would be free to continue helping Mark with his homework and to drive him and Christa to their various activities.

For Terry, it had been a time of immense personal and physical growth. I have never seen one person make such great strides in such a short period of time; and it had been so very exciting for me to see his new life unfold before my very eyes through his letters.

The trip marked another milestone for Tara. For the first time she was able to push her torso up off the floor completely unaided. She could get up on her elbows and almost to her knees—the closest thing to a hands-and-knees position she had ever been able to attain without assistance.

In fact, she was getting up so high when she crawled that it slowed her down considerably. Her ultimate goal for the three months had been to crawl 100 feet in ten minutes. Her crawling distance had been increased from ten feet the first week to twenty feet the second week, forty feet the third week, eighty feet the fourth week and one hundred feet the fifth week. From then on, the distance Tara crawled at a time remained constant at one hundred feet.

It was hoped that the increased time spent in crawling would increase the speed with which

Tara performed this grueling exercise. However, this did not materialize. Tara began her program there by crawling the ten feet in an average of three minutes. At the end of the three months, Tara was averaging 100 feet in thirty minutes or three minutes for every ten feet.

So, in that respect only, the trip was a failure. We didn't consider it so for three reasons, however. First of all, Tara was definitely making progress toward hands and knees creeping. Secondly, it helped us to decide to begin to look elsewhere for treatment methods for Tara. In the third place, the trip had been emotionally good for Tara and Terry, and for our family.

We were glad we had sent Tara to Philadelphia, but we were awfully anxious to have her back home again. Terry and Tara were ready to be reunited with their loved ones in California, but they had made so many special friends during their stay that leave-taking proved to be a rather painful experience for them. Tara just cried and cried when she had to say good-bye to her friend Laurie Longenecker.

Pastor Murray asked Terry to give his testimony during worship services the Sunday before they were to leave.

"We have known and loved Tara Nason from some previous visits to the church," Chuck began, "but in the last three months we have come to know Terry Patané, a very special friend of Tara's. Terry not only came into our lives, but for those of us who know him, he quickly came into our hearts. I really love that man. He has inspired me so much by his faith in Christ and his willingness to be used as the Lord led him."

Terry had joined Pastor Murray at the pulpit and, with a lump in his throat, tried to explain what the three months had meant to him. "One thing that's been foremost in my mind these past three months has been the feeling of the nearness of God. As a Christian, I know that God is always near and that he's usually nearest when we're not aware of it. But for the first time in my Christian life, I've really felt his nearness in a very special way, and that's what has really strengthened me through all of this. I have really grown—not only as a Christian, but as a person. All the love and kindness that you have given Tara and me have been part of that process of growth within me, and I just want to thank each and every one of you for what you've given us. God bless you!"

The church held a reception for Terry and Tara following the service and expressed their love by giving Terry a watch and Tara some jewelry. The deacons also voted to give Tara a new wheelchair, which she desperately needed, having outgrown her first one. Shortly before their departure, Oreland Presbyterian Church scheduled a day of prayer especially for Tara. The sanctuary was kept open all day for friends to come and offer prayers for her healing.

In a subsequent letter to Terry, Pastor Murray further expressed his feelings: "Terry, it is simply impossible to tell you how much we appreciate all that you, Tara, Mike and Donna, Dr. Schuller, and the whole Hour of Power ministry have meant to this church. I believe we are much closer to God and much more effective for the Lord because our lives have been touched by yours."

Dr. Schuller often says, "Only God can count the apples in a seed." Terry and Tara planted many seeds in Philadelphia during their brief stay, and only God knows the far-reaching consequences of their visit. It is like little ripples of God's love, growing and expanding into ever-widening circles throughout eternity.

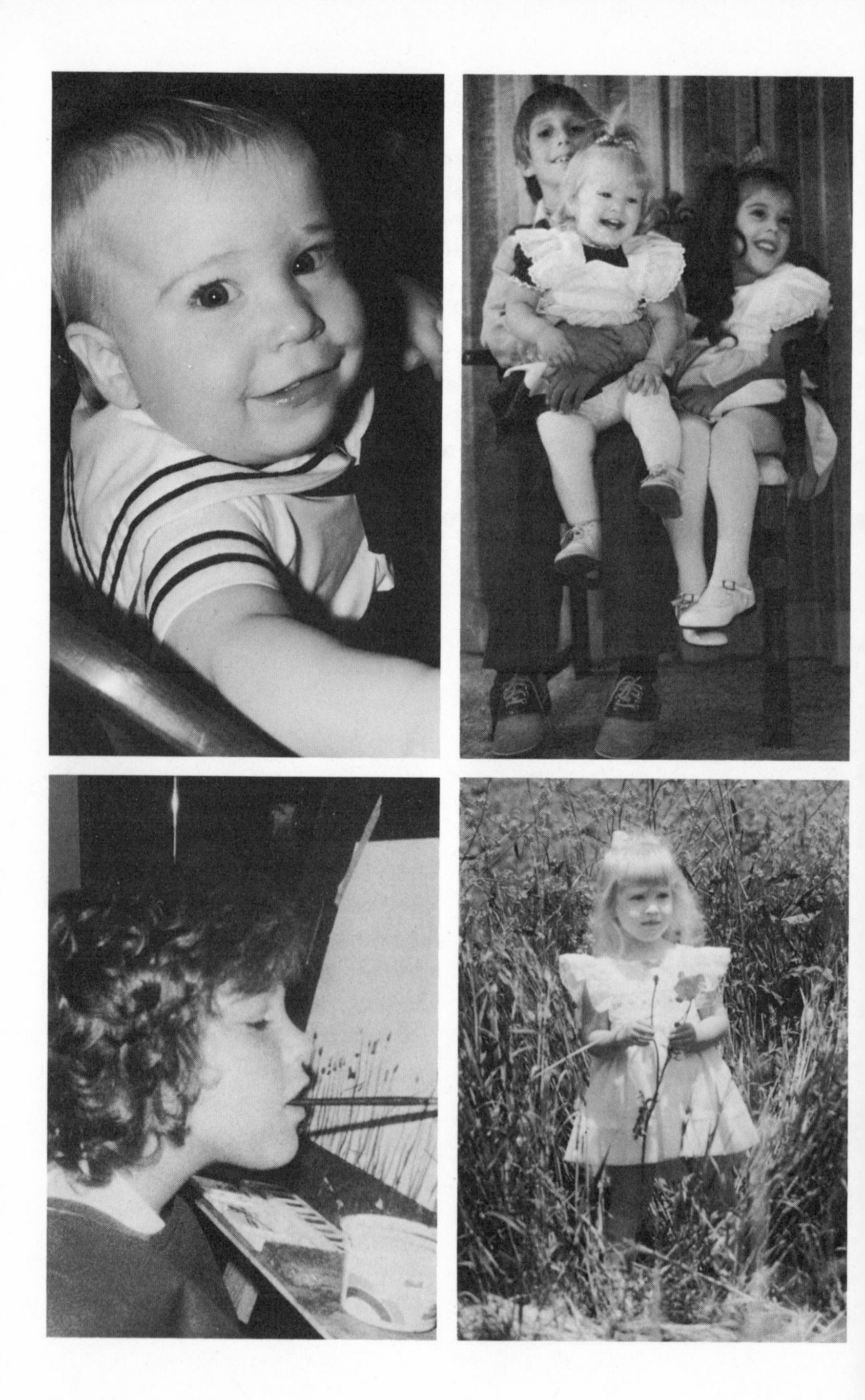

CHAPTER TWELVE
Children of Hopes and Dreams

Back in November, Christa had told some visitors to our home, “We’re going to have a loving Christmas, because Tara’s going to be home.” This turned out to be quite prophetic, because our lives were much brighter and fuller once our family circle was complete again.

During Tara’s absence, Mike wrote a poem about her while away on one of his many business trips.

I have a daughter. Her name is Tara.
She cannot walk and she cannot write.
She cannot play and she cannot dance.
But—she can smile and she can laugh.
She can talk and she can love.
Because—God made her a child of Hopes and Dreams.

We were very glad to have our child of hopes and dreams back home again!

Tara entered school with characteristic enthusiasm, and her teacher, Maxine, was delighted that she had not forgotten all she had learned the previous year. Tara's typing was of great importance, because here was a way for her to express herself on paper. Here also, we hope, is the key for her to learn how to read. We just praised God that she had remembered the keyboard after not having seen it for six months.

In fact, she did so well in her first days back at school that Maxine was encouraged enough to ask for a special new typewriter for her. Tara had been typing on a portable electric one that actually belonged to her gregarious teacher. To our surprise, the school district approved the immediate purchase of a custom Olympia typewriter with primary print and all the necessary extras so that Tara could turn it on and off herself, and put in and center the paper, and return the carriage to the margin at the end of a line.

I went in to school one day to see her and had to smile at the strange sight that greeted me. There was a little girl in a wheelchair, pushed up to a table on which sat a large typewriter. Her head was encased in a big brown synthetic fur hat, an old one of Maxine's which she had brought in to keep the headgear from slipping around on Tara's soft, shiny hair.

Over the hat sat the actual headgear itself, an outer-space-looking contraption fashioned of chrome and self-adhering velcro straps with a long metal pointer extending from the top of Tara's head right down between her eyes. Tara sat engrossed in her work, bobbing her head up and down as she hit the keys with the tip of the pointer.

"Mommy," she called excitedly when she caught sight of me, "come see what I can do!" She proceeded to give me a demonstration of just how she could operate her typewriter all by herself. She was so proud and had such a great sense of accomplishment; it was wonderful to see.

She now types a letter to someone everyday, either to one of her school friends or to some member of the family. She puts little stickers on the paper to make it look like stationery, and all the children at school love to receive mail from Tara. She has learned to spell and type many words and to arrange these words together in sentences.

The children in Tara's class were making deviled eggs the other day. Tara took the knife in her mouth and neatly halved a dozen hard-boiled eggs. Then she put a fork in her mouth and took all the yolks out of the eggs and put them into a bowl for her classmates to mash.

Maxine had fixed her an easel with watercolors, and Tara learned how to paint with a brush attached to her headgear. She can rinse the brush after each color so that the colors do not run and mix.

Without giving up, Tara is learning to work with what she has going for her right now. She is learning not to waste her time feeling sorry for what she has lost or dreaming of what she may someday have. Instead, she is learning to accept and to be thankful for the way she is and to make the best possible use of her present capabilities, while at the same time working to make them better. She is finally learning to find the balance for her life that is so essential to happiness, and we are so very thankful.

There are yet other plans on the horizon for Tara, and we will not stop until we have explored every possibility. Medical science is learning more about the complexities of the brain every day. With God's help, maybe someday an answer will be found for all the Taras of the world.

A few years ago, Dr. Irving Cooper, a prominent neurosurgeon in New York, began pioneering work in implanting brain pacemakers. The pacemaker consists, basically, of a series of electrodes embedded in a plastic mesh, surgically placed on the cerebellum. This is an area of the brain located near the base of the skull. The electrodes are connected by a copper wire to a receiver unit which is sewn into the chest of the user. A power source outside of the body transmits power to the receiver, which in turn electronically stimulates the brain tissue, modifying the muscle spasms that occur with crippling effect in nerve-muscle afflictions.

Originally used as an aid to help control seizures in epileptics, the pacemaker has proved somewhat successful in reducing spasticity in children like Tara. Her extreme rigidity is one of the main reasons why Tara cannot move her body as she would like. It is not that she is paralyzed or unable to feel or completely lacking in coordination; it is simply that she is too stiff to move.

We have been aware of the brain pacemaker since Tara was four years old, when we took her to see Dr. Cooper at St. Barnabas Hospital in New York City. At that time, he was not recommending the procedure for anyone under twelve years of age. However, since that time the surgery has been perfected considerably, and there are several neurosurgeons all across the country who perform the operation on children of all ages.

Surgery frightens me, and I have wanted to avoid it at all costs in our treatment of Tara. But during her trip to Philadelphia, I saw something that made me change my mind.

A little five-year-old boy who lives near us, Kevin Berry, had a brain pacemaker surgically implanted at the age of four. One day when I was feeling especially brave, I made an appointment to go over and see Kevin and his mother. A friend of mine, Sue Hutchinson, whose son Bobby is also brain-injured, came too. Kevin is a tiny little boy with a very big smile. Prior to receiving the pacemaker, he had done very little in his four short years but cry the brain cry I remembered so well from Tara. He made no other sounds, not even baby talk, and was not actually able to move. He had had no use of his hands whatsoever and had kept them tightly closed, thumbs inside his little fists, just as Tara usually does.

His mother explained to me that within a few months following his surgery, Kevin's brain cry gradually disappeared altogether. He began to make sounds and could even speak a few words. Then she handed him a small box of raisins, and I watched with astonished joy as he opened it and one by one picked out the raisins with his thumb and forefinger and put them in his mouth.

My eyes filled with tears, and I thought it was one of the most beautiful sights I had ever seen. I looked over at Sue and saw the tears well up and trickle down her cheeks, and I knew we were both thinking the same thing. "Dear God, please! If only my child could use his fingers like that!"

Mrs. Berry put Kevin down on the floor, and he pushed easily up onto his hands and knees. I gasped. Sue trembled. Here was a child who had had practically no therapy and yet could function in a way far superior to our children, who had received years of patterning.

Right then and there I decided for sure that I wanted Tara to have the brain pacemaker surgery. Mike, who is not as timid a soul as I am, had been in favor of the operation for some time. Now that I had stopped dragging my feet, we knew the time had come for action.

Mike and I both feel at peace that this is what the Lord wants for Tara right now, and we are excited about her upcoming surgery. It is so hard to keep the balance between our wildest hopes and our worst fears, but we are trying. We realize that Tara could so benefit from the pacemaker that she might be walking soon. We also know that it is entirely possible that it might do practically nothing for her whatsoever. Then again, it might so relieve her spasticity that she could begin to have limited function which could be improved upon with therapy. Realistically, it is for this that we are actually hoping. All we can do is pray and wait upon the Lord. We are hoping to have thousands of people praying for a successful outcome to the surgery, and we are trusting God to do what is ultimately best for Tara.

Mark also is really coming into his own. He has matured so much this past year, and at twelve is fast becoming a young man. His soccer team came in first place in their division this year, and now Mark is very busy roller skating. We have a beautiful indoor rink near our home, and Mark has his own skates. He spends much of his spare time there, working off some of his excess energy and making new friends.

With his paper route, he earned enough money to pay for over half of a ten-speed bicycle he had wanted for a long time. It has taken him longer than most; and he still, like all children his age, has a long way to go, but he is beginning to put his life together.

Little Christa continues to delight us every day with her very normalcy. The things other parents take for granted are so thrilling for us. She sits still and watches television, she colors by the hour—she even stays within the lines of the pictures in her coloring books! She puts puzzles together, she likes to print letters, and is learning to write her name. She is sweet and curious and eager. I wish I could tell every parent what a miracle it is to have a child who can do all these things! When I was expecting Christa, I prayed so earnestly to God about the baby I was carrying. I was bold and asked him specifically for many different characteristics and attributes for this child. It is still hard for me to believe it, but he has answered every request I made; and as Christa's life unfolds, I see more and more of the little girl of my dreams.

She is unusually sensitive in spiritual matters, and loves to talk and sing about Jesus. One night when she was three and a half, I decided to broach the subject of salvation with her. I wanted to be sure she realized that Jesus died for her and that he wanted to be her best friend forever.

I began talking about God's love for her in a very simple, straightforward way. But she stopped me dead in my tracks! "Mommy," she said, rolling those big blue eyes toward me, "I already have Jesus in my heart. Don't you know that?" I questioned her carefully and sure enough, she had received Christ already, through prayer. I was so happy that my Christa knew my Savior in a personal way, but I couldn't help but feel sad for having missed out on such a special moment with my daughter.

Our family just recently celebrated a very special day—baby Shannon's first birthday. It was a day of praise and thanksgiving for the life of this dear little boy. A chubby little whirlwind with big, round blue eyes, four teeth, and a soft down of blond hair, Shannon is a constantly unfolding miracle.

Every few months a public health nurse comes to our home to test him developmentally. And he has never failed to be right on schedule! So far there appear to be no signs of any brain damage whatsoever. He likes to play with his brother and sisters and to creep everywhere on his hands and knees. He likes to stand up and walk around the furniture and to play peek-a-boo. He likes to get into everything he's not supposed to, and he cries "ma ma" when he is unhappy. He doesn't like getting his face washed, getting his diapers changed, or being told he can't play with the pretty things on Mommy's coffee table.

In short, he's just about like all other twelve-month-old babies—the ones who didn't suffer respiratory arrest shortly after birth. God is so good!

What does the future hold for our family? Laughter and tears? Probably. Love and loneliness? I imagine. But thank God, I don't have to worry about that. God tells me that he'll take care of tomorrow. And I believe him. "Therefore do not be anxious for tomorrow; for tomorrow will care for itself. Each day has enough trouble of its own" (Matthew 6:34).

One day not too long ago, Mike and I went shopping for a new desk for his office. We picked one out but didn't buy it at that time. A few days later, Mike had his secretary, Marge, call the store and place the order. The older gentleman who had helped us remembered our visit. "You know," he told Marge, "I've worked here a long time and have helped many executives pick out their office furniture, but I've never seen a couple with such peace about them as that one. That young man knew who he was and where he was going. What's his business?"

Marge explained to him that Mike is producer

of Hour of Power and told him a little about this dynamic Christian television program. She also told him a little about our special family.

He was utterly amazed. "I'm going to watch that program," he said. "There's got to be something special there. I'd like to have that kind of peace."

What kind of peace is it? It's God's peace. The peace that "passes all understanding." Certainly there is little about our earthly circumstances that would produce peace. But God's peace is the peace in the midst of the storm.

Sometimes I feel that I am so confused and bewildered about my life, with my emotions playing tug-of-war in a hundred different directions. And yet somehow, in the middle of interior and exterior pandemonium, I know that God loves me and will never leave me alone. I know that in the end, things will work out all right. I can trust my Lord to see me through life's stormy sea and bring me at last into the calm, crystal blue waters of eternity. It makes the struggle all seem so worthwhile, and puts my heart at rest.

One night it was raining quite hard outside. Tara was frightened, and I was trying to console her. We talked about Jesus.

"Don't be afraid, Tara," I said. "You know Jesus is with you. You know how much he loves you and that he plans everything for your good."

"I know, Mommy," she said, beginning to brighten a little.

"In fact," I said, "Jesus is right here in your

bed, and he's going to stay with you all night. He won't sleep like you will, because he doesn't need to. He'll stay awake and watch over you and care for you."

Tara blinked back her tears and broke into a big smile. "Really?" she asked. "Will Jesus stay in your bed tonight too and take care of you and Daddy?"

"Yes, he sure will," I promised.

"Is he going to stay in Christa's bed, too?"

"Yes, honey, he'll be with Christa all night."

I could almost see the wheels begin to turn inside Tara's head. She was thinking of Christa, who was a baby at the time, sleeping in her little crib. "But, Mommy," she said, "will Jesus fit?"

How wonderful that we have a God big enough to flash through the sky in a streak of lightning, yet small enough to fit inside a baby's crib. He is a supernatural God who isn't limited by time and space . . . who can be everywhere and know everything in the universe all at the same time . . . a God who is so incomparably powerful that he created worlds we will never see, and yet is so intimately involved with each of us that at any given time he knows the exact number of hairs on each of our heads.

Hallelujah!